MENTAL

Studies in Consciousness

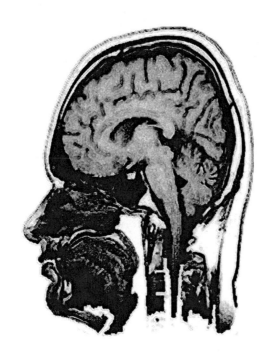

BY

UPTON SINCLAIR

edited by Dr. Jane Ma'ati Smith

INTRODUCTION

MR. UPTON SINCLAIR needs no introduction to the public as a fearless, honest, and critical student of public affairs. But in the present book he has with characteristic courage entered a new field, one in which reputations are more easily lost than made, the field of Psychic Research. When he does me the honor to ask me to write a few words of introduction to this book, a refusal would imply on my part a lack either of courage or of due sense of scientific responsibility, I have long been keenly interested in this field; and it is not necessary to hold that the researches of the past fifty years have brought any solidly established conclusions in order to feel sure that further research is very much worth while. Even if the results of such research should in the end prove wholly negative that would be a result of no small importance; for from many points of view it is urgently to be wished that we may know where we stand in this question of the reality of alleged supernormal phenomena. In discussing this question recently with a small group of scientific men, one of them (who is perhaps the most prominent and influential of American psychologists) seemed to feel that the whole problem was settled in the negative when he asserted that at the present time no American psychologist of standing took any interest in this field. I do not know whether he meant to deny my Americanism or my standing, neither of which I can establish. But his remark if it were true, would not in any degree support his conclusion; it would rather be a grave reproach to American psychologists. Happily it is possible to name several younger American psychologists who are keenly interested in the problem of telepathy.

And it is with experiments in telepathy that Mr. Sinclair's book is chiefly concerned. In this part, as in other parts, of the field of Psychic Research, progress must largely depend upon such work by intelligent educated laymen or amateurs as is here reported. For facility in obtaining seemingly supernormal phenomena seems to be of rare and sporadic occurrence; and it is the duty of men of science to give whatever encouragement and sympathetic support may be possible to all amateurs who find themselves in a position to observe and carefully and honestly to study such phenomena.

Mrs. Sinclair would seem to be one of the rare persons who have telepathic power in a marked degree and perhaps other supernormal powers. The experiments in telepathy, as reported in the pages of this book, were so remarkably successful as to rank among the very best hitherto reported. The degree of success and the conditions of experiment were such that we can reject them as conclusive evidence of some mode of communication not at present explicable in accepted scientific terms only by assuming that Mr. and Mrs. Sinclair either are grossly stupid, incompetent and careless persons or have deliberately entered upon a conspiracy to deceive the public in a most heartless and reprehensible fashion. I have unfortunately no intimate personal knowledge of Mr. and Mrs. Sinclair; but I am acquainted with some of Mr. Sinclair's earlier publications; and that acquaintance suffices to convince me, as it should convince any impartial reader, that he is an able and sincere man with a strong sense of right and wrong and of individual responsibility. His record and his writings should secure a wide and respectful hearing for what he has to tell us in the following pages.

Mrs. Sinclair's account of her condition during successful experiments seems to me particularly interesting; for it falls into line with what has been observed by several other workers; namely, they report that a peculiar passive mental state or attitude seems to be a highly favorable, if not an essential, condition of telepathic communication. It would seem that if the faint and unusual telepathic processes are to manifest themselves, the track of the mind must be kept clear of other traffic.

Other experiments reported in the book seem to imply some supernormal power of perception of physical things such as is commonly called clairvoyance. It is natural and logical that alleged instances of clairvoyance should have from most of us a reception even more skeptical than that we accord to telepathic claims. After all, a mind at work is an active agent of whose nature and activity our knowledge is very imperfect; and science furnishes us no good reasons for denying that its activity may affect another mind in some fashion utterly obscure to us. But when an experimenter seems to have large success in reading printed words shut in a thick-walled box, words whose identity is unknown to any human being, we seem to be more nearly in a position to assert positively—That cannot occur! For we do seem to know with very fair completeness the possibilities of influence extending from the printed word to the experimenter; and under the conditions all such possibilities seem surely excluded. Yet here also we must keep the open mind, gather the facts, however unintelligible they may seem at present, repeating observations under varied conditions.

And Mrs. Sinclair's clairvoyant successes do not stand alone. They are in line with the many successful "book-tests" recorded of recent years by competent workers of the English Society for Psychical Research, as well as with many other less carefully observed and recorded incidents.

Mr. Sinclair's book will amply justify itself if it shall lead a few (let us say two per cent) of his readers to undertake carefully and critically experiments similar to those which he has so vividly described.

William McDougall

DUKE UNIVERSITY, N. C.
September, 1929.

MENTAL RADIO

I

IF you were born as long as fifty years ago, you can remember a time when the test of a sound, common-sense mind was refusing to fool with "new-fangled notions." Without exactly putting it into a formula, people took it for granted that truth was known and familiar, and anything that was not known and familiar was nonsense. In my boyhood, the funniest joke in the world was a "flying machine man"; and when my mother took up a notion about "germs" getting into you and making you sick, my father made it a theme for no end of domestic wit. Even as late as twenty years ago, when I wanted to write a play based on the idea that men might some day be able to make a human voice audible to groups of people all over America, my friends assured me that I could not interest the public in such a fantastic notion.

Among the objects of scorn, in my boyhood, was what we called "superstition"; and we made the term include, not merely the notion that the number thirteen brought you bad luck; not merely a belief in witches, ghosts and goblins, but also a belief in any strange phenomena of the mind which we did not understand. We knew about hypnotism, because we had seen stage performances, and were in the midst of reading a naughty book called "Trilby"; but such things as trance mediumship, automatic writing, table-tapping, telekinesis, telepathy and clairvoyance—we didn't know these long names, but if such ideas were explained to us, we knew right away that it was "all nonsense."

In my youth I had the experience of meeting a scholarly Unitarian clergyman, the Rev. Minot J. Savage of New York, who assured me quite seriously that he had seen and talked with ghosts. He didn't convince me, but he sowed the seed of curiosity in my mind, and I began reading books on psychic research. From first to last, I have read hundreds of volumes; always interested, and always uncertain—an uncomfortable mental state. The evidence in support of telepathy came to seem to me conclusive, yet it never quite became real to me. The consequences of belief would be so tremendous, the changes it would make in my view of the universe so revolutionary, that I didn't believe, even when I said I did.

But for thirty years the subject has been among the things I hoped to know about; and, as it happened, fate was planning to favor me. It sent me a wife who became interested, and who not merely investigated telepathy, but learned to practice it. For the past three years I have been watching this work, day by day and night by night, in our home. So at last I can say that I am no longer guessing. Now I really. know. I am going to tell you about it, and hope to convince you; but regardless of what anybody can say, there will never again be a doubt about it in my mind. I KNOW!

II

TELEPATHY, or mind-reading: that is to say, can one human mind communicate with another human mind, except by the sense channels ordinarily known and used—seeing, hearing, feeling, tasting and touching? Can a thought or image in one mind be sent directly to another mind and there reproduced and recognized? If this can be done, how is it done? Is it some kind of vibration, going out from the brain, like radio broadcasting? Or is it some contact with a deeper level of mind, as bubbles on a stream have contact with the water of the stream? And if this power exists, can it be developed and used? Is it something that manifests itself now and then, like a lightning flash, over which we have no control? Or can we make the energy and store it, and use it regularly, as we have learned to do with the lightning which Franklin brought from the clouds?

These are the questions; and the answers, as well as I can summarize them, are as follows: Telepathy is real; it does happen. Whatever may be the nature of the force, it has nothing to do with distance, for it works exactly as well over forty miles as over thirty feet. And while it may be spontaneous and may depend upon a special endowment, it can be cultivated and used deliberately, as any other object of study, in physics and chemistry. The essential in this training is an art of mental concentration and autosuggestion, which can be learned. I am going to tell you not merely what you can do, but how you can do it, so that if you have patience and real interest, you can make your own contribution to knowledge.

Starting the subject, I am like the wandering book-agent or peddler who taps on your door and gets you to open it, and has to speak quickly and persuasively, putting his best goods foremost. Your prejudice is against this idea; and if you are one of my old-time readers, you are a little shocked to find me taking up a new and unexpected line of activity. You have come, after thirty years, to the position where you allow me to be one kind of "crank," but you won't stand for two kinds. So let me come straight to the point— open up my pack, pull out my choicest wares, and catch your attention with them if I can.

Here is a drawing of a table-fork. It was done with a lead-pencil on a sheet of ruled paper, which has been photographed, and then reproduced in the ordinary way. You note that it bears a signature and a date (fig. 1):

Fig. 1

This drawing was produced by my brother-in-law, Robert L. Irwin, a young business man, and no kind of "crank," under the following circumstances. He was sitting in a room in his home in Pasadena at a specified hour, eleven-thirty in the morning of July 13, 1928, having agreed to make a drawing of any object he might select, at random, and then to sit gazing at it, concentrating his entire attention upon it for a period of from fifteen to twenty minutes.

At the same agreed hour, eleven-thirty in the morning of July 13, 1928, my wife was lying on the couch in her study, in our home in Long Beach, forty miles away by the road. She was in semi-darkness, with her eyes closed; employing a system of mental concentration which she has been practicing off and on for several years, and mentally suggesting to her subconscious mind to bring her whatever was in the mind of her brother-in-law. Having become satisfied that the image which came to her mind was the correct one—because it persisted, and came back again and again—she sat up and took pencil and paper and wrote the date, and six words, as follows (fig. 1a):

July 13, 1428
See a table
fork. Nothing
else.

Fig. 1a

A day or two later we drove to Pasadena, and then in the presence of Bob and his wife, the drawing and writing were produced and compared. I have in my possession affidavits from Bob, his wife, and my wife, to the effect that the drawing and writing were produced in this way. Later in this book I shall present four other pairs of drawings, made in the same way, three of them equally successful.

Second case. Here is a drawing (fig. 2), and below it a set of five drawings (fig. 2a):

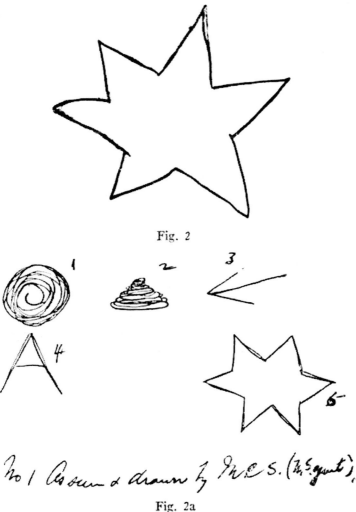

Fig. 2

Fig. 2a

The above drawings were produced under the following circumstances. The single drawing (fig. 2) was made by me in my study at my home. I was alone, and the door was closed before the drawing was made, and was not opened until the test was concluded. Having made the drawing, I held it before me and concentrated upon it for a period of five or ten minutes.

The five drawings (fig. 2a) were produced by my wife, who was lying on the couch in her study, some thirty feet away from me, with the door closed between us. The only words spoken were as follows: when I was ready to make my drawing, I called, "All right," and when she had completed her drawings, she called, "All right" — whereupon I opened the door and took my drawing to her and we compared them. I found that in addition to the five little pictures, she had written some explanation of how she came to draw them. This I shall quote and discuss later on. I shall also tell about six other pairs of drawings, produced in this same way.

Third case: another drawing (fig. 3a), produced under the following circumstances. My wife went upstairs, and shut the door which is at the top of the stairway. I went on tip-toe to a cupboard in a downstairs room and took from a shelf a red electric-light bulb—it having been agreed that I should select any small article, of which there were certainly many hundreds in our home. I wrapped this bulb in several thicknesses of newspaper, and put it, so wrapped, in a shoe-box, and wrapped the shoe-box in a whole newspaper, and tied it tightly with a string. I then called my wife and she came downstairs, and lay on her couch and put the box on her body, over the solar plexus. I sat watching, and never took my eyes from her, nor did I speak a word during the test. Finally she sat up, and made her drawing, with the written comment, and handed it to me. Every word of the comment, as well as the drawing, was produced before I said a word, and the drawing and writing as here reproduced have not been touched or altered in any way (fig. 3a):

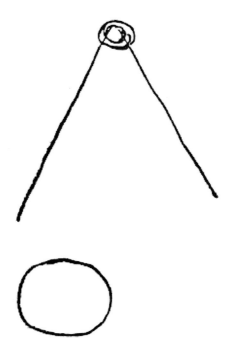

Fig. 3a

The text of my wife's written comment is as follows:

"First see round glass. Guess nose glasses? No. Then comes V shape again with a 'button' in top. Button stands out from object. This round top is of different color from lower part. It is light color, the other part is dark."

To avoid any possible misunderstanding, perhaps I should state that the question and answer in the above were my wife's description of her own mental process, and do not represent a question asked of me. She did not "guess" aloud, nor did either of us speak a single word during this test, except the single word, "Ready," to call my wife downstairs.

The next drawings were produced in the following manner. The one at the top (fig. 4) was drawn by me alone in my study, and was one of nine, all made at the same time, and with no restriction upon what I should draw—anything that came into my head.

Having made the nine drawings, I wrapped each one in a separate sheet of green paper, to make it absolutely invisible, and put each one in a plain envelope and sealed it, and then took the nine sealed envelopes and laid them on the table by my wife's couch. My wife then took one of them and placed it

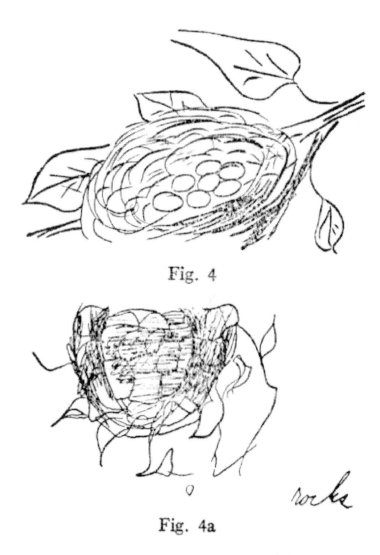

Fig. 4

Fig. 4a

over her solar plexus, and lay in her state of concentration, while I sat watching her, at her insistence, in order to make the evidence more convincing. Having received what she considered a convincing telepathic "message," or image of the contents of the envelope, she sat up and made her sketch (fig. 4a) on a pad of paper.

The essence of our procedure is this: that never did she see my drawing until hers was completed and her descriptive words written; that I spoke no word and made no comment until after this was done; and that the drawings presented here are in every case exactly what I drew, and the corresponding drawing is exactly what my wife drew, with no change or addition whatsoever. In the case of this particular pair, my wife wrote: "Inside of rock well with vines climbing on outside." Such was her guess as to the drawing, which I had meant for a bird's nest surrounded by leaves; but you see that the two drawings are for practical purposes identical.

Many tests have been made, by each of the different methods above outlined, and the results will be given and explained in these pages. The method of attempting to reproduce little drawings was used more than any other, simply because it proved the most convenient; it could be done at a moment's notice, and so fitted into our busy lives. The procedure was varied in a few details to save time and trouble, as I shall later explain, but the essential feature remains unchanged: I make a set of drawings, and my wife takes them one by one and attempts to reproduce them without having seen them. Here are a few samples, chosen at random because of their picturesque character. If my wife wrote anything on the drawing, I add it as "comment"; and you are to understand here, and for the rest of this book, that "comment" means the exact words which she wrote *before* she saw my drawing. Often there will be parts of this "comment" visible in the photograph. I give it all in print. Note that drawings 1, 2, 3, etc., are mine, while la, 2a, 3a, etc., are my wife's.

In the case of my drawing numbered five, my wife's comment was: "Knight's helmet."

On figure 6, the comment was: "Desert scene, camel, ostrich, then below"—and the drawing in figure 6a. On the reverse side of the page is further comment: "This came in fragments, as if I saw it being drawn by invisible pencil."

Fig. 5

Fig. 5a

Fig. 6

Fig. 6a

14

And here is a pair with no comment, and none needed (fig. 7, 7a):

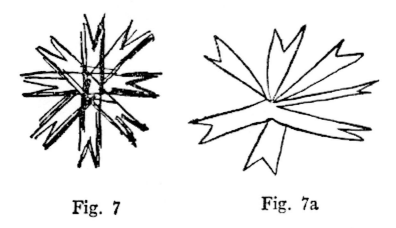

Fig. 7   Fig. 7a

On the following, also, no comment was written (fig. 8, 8a):

Fig. 8   Fig. 8a

Fig. 9

Fig. 9a

I drew figure 9, and my wife drew 9a, a striking success, and wrote the comment: "May be elephant's snout—but anyway it is some kind of a running animal. Long thing like rope flung out in front of him."

Next, a series of three pairs, which, as it happened, were done one after the other, numbers three, four and five in the twenty-third series of my drawings. They are selected in part because they are amusing. First, I tried to draw a bat, from vague memories of boyhood days when they used to fly into the ball-rooms at Virginia springs hotels, and have to be massacred with brooms, because it

16

was believed that they sought to tangle themselves in the hair of the ladies (fig. 10, 10a):

Fig. 10

Fig. 10a

My wife's comment on the above reads: "Big insect. I know this is right because it moves his legs as if flying. Beetle working its legs. Legs in motion!"

And next, my effort at a Chinese mandarin (fig. 11, 11a):

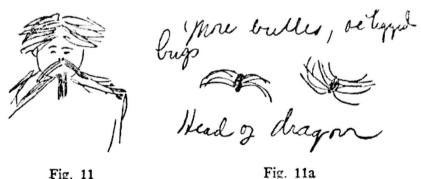

Fig. 11   Fig. 11a

The comment reads: "More beetles, or legged bugs"—and she draws the mustaches of the mandarin and his hair. "Head of dragon

with big mouth. See also a part of his body—in front, or shoulders."
The association of mandarins with dragons is obvious.

And finally, my effort at a boy's foot and roller-skate, which
undergoes a strange telepathic transformation. I have put it upside
down for easier comparison (fig. 12, 12a):

Fig. 12

Fig. 12a

The comment, complete, reads: "Profile of head and neck of animal—lion or dog—a muzzle. Maybe pig snout."

The above are samples of our successes. Altogether, of such drawings, 38 were prepared by my secretary, while I made 252, a total of 290. I have classified the drawings to the best of my ability into three groups: successes, partial successes, and failures. The partial successes are those drawings which contain some easily recognized element of the original drawing: such as, for example, the last one above. The profile of a pig's head is not a roller skate, but when you compare the drawings, you see that in my wife's first sketch the eyes resemble the wheels of the roller-skates, and in her second sketch the snout resembles my shoe-tip; also there is a general similarity of outline, which is what she most commonly gets.

In the 290 drawings, the total of successes is 65, which is roughly 23 per cent. The total of partial successes is 155, which is 53 per cent. The total of failures is 70, which is 24 per cent. I asked some mathematician friends to work out the probabilities on the above results, but I found that the problem was too complicated. Who could estimate how many possible objects there were, which might come into my head to be drawn? Any time the supply ran short, I would pick up a magazine, and in the advertising pages find a score of new drawings to imitate. Again, very few of the drawings were simple. We began with such things as a circle, a square, a cross, a number or a letter; but soon we were doing Chinese mandarins with long mustaches, and puppies chasing a string. Each of these drawings has many different features; and what mathematician could count the number of these features, and the chances of reproducing them?

It is a matter to be judged by common sense. It seems to me any one must agree that the chances of the twelve drawings so far shown having been reproduced by accident is too great to be worth considering. A million years would not be enough for such a set of coincidences.

III

MUCH of the evidence which I am using rests upon the good faith of Mary Craig Sinclair; so, before we go further, I ask your permission to introduce her. She is a daughter of the far South; her father a retired planter, bank president and judge, of Mississippi. The fates endowed his oldest child with the blessings of beauty, health, wealth and wisdom—and then spoiled it, by adding a curse in the shape of a too tender heart. The griefs of other people overwhelm Craig like a suffocation. Strangers take one glance at her, and instantly decide that here is one who will "understand." I have seen her go into a store to buy a piece of ribbon, and come out with tears in her eyes, because of a tragic story which some clerk was moved to pour out to her, all in a moment, without provocation.

She has always said that she "gets" the feelings of people, not by their words, but by intuition. But she never paid any attention to this gift; never associated it with "psychic" matters. She was always too busy, first with eight younger brothers and sisters, and then with the practical affairs of an unpractical author-husband.

Early in childhood, things like this would happen: her mother would say to a little negro servant, "Go and find Miss Mary Craig"; but before the boy could start, Craig would know that her mother wanted her, and would be on the way. This might, of course, have been coincidence; if it stood alone, it would have no value. But the same thing happened with dreams. Craig dreamed there was a needle in her bed, and woke up and looked for it in vain; in the morning she told her mother, who slept in another room. The mother said: "How strange! I dreamed the same thing, and I woke up and really found one!"

Of her young ladyhood, Craig tells this story, one of many: Driving with a girl friend, miles from home, she suddenly remarked: "Let's go home; Mr. B is there." Now this was a place to which Mr. B had never come; it was three hundred miles from his town. But Craig said: "I have just had an impression of him, sitting on our front porch." Going home, they found him there.

Another instance, of more recent date. Shortly after our coming to California, my wife all at once became greatly worried about Jack London; she insisted that he was in terrible mental distress. As it happened, George Sterling had told us much about Jack's troubles, but these were of old standing, and there was nothing to account for the sudden notion which my wife took up on a certain day. We had a lot of conversation about it; I offered to take her to the London ranch, but she said she would not attempt to meddle in the affairs of a married man, unless at his wife's request. I made the laughing suggestion that she go alone, in the guise of a gypsy fortune-teller—a rôle which in her young ladyhood she had played with social éclat. Two days later we read that Jack London was dead, and very soon came letters from George Sterling, telling us that he had taken his own life. This, again, might be coincidence; if it stood alone I would attach no importance to it. But taken with this mass of evidence, it has a share of weight.

When we were married, seventeen years ago, we spent some time in England, and there we met a woman physician, interested in "mental healing," and full of ideas about "psychic" things. Both Craig and I were in need of healing, having been through a siege of trouble.

Craig was suffering with intense headaches, something hitherto unknown in her life; while I had an ancient problem of indigestion, caused by excess of brain work and lack of body work. We began to experiment with healing by the "laying on of hands"—without knowing anything about it, just groping in the dark. I found that I could cure Craig's headaches—and get them myself; while she found that she could take my indigestion, a trouble she had never known hitherto. Each of us was willing to take the other's pains, but neither was willing to give them, so our experiments came to a halt.

We forgot the whole subject for more than ten years. I was busy trying to reform America; while Craig was of the most intensely materialistic convictions. Her early experiences of evangelical religion had repelled her so violently that everything suggestive of "spirituality" was repugnant to her. Never was a woman more "practical," more centered upon the here and now, the things which can be seen and touched. I do not go into details about this, but I want to make it as emphatic as possible, for the light it throws upon her attitude and disposition.

But shortly after the age of forty, her custom of carrying the troubles of all who were near her resulted in a breakdown of health. A story of suffering needless to go into: suffice it that she had many ills to experiment upon, and mental control became suddenly a matter of life and death. In the course of the last five or six years Craig has acquired a fair-sized library of books on the mind, both orthodox scientific, and "crank." She has sat up half the night studying, marking passages and making notes, seeking to reconcile various doctrines, to know what the mind really is, and how it works, and what can be done with it. Always it was a practical problem: things had to work. If now she believes anything, rest assured that it is because she has tried it out in the crucibles of pain, and proved it in her daily regimen.

She was not content to see psychic phenomena produced by other persons. Even though authorities warned her that trances might be dangerous, and that *rapport* with others might lead to dissociations of personality—even so, she had to find out for herself. A hundred times in the course of the experiments of which I am going to tell, she has turned to me, saying: "Can you think of any way this can be chance? What can I do to make it more sure?" When I said, the other night: "This settles it for me. I am going to write the story," her reply was, "Wait a while!" She wants to do more experimenting; but I think that enough is enough.

IV

Two years ago Craig and I heard of a "psychic," a young foreigner who was astounding physicians of Southern California, performing feats so completely beyond their understanding that they were content to watch without trying to understand. We went to see this young man, and befriended him; he came to our home every day, and his strange demonstrations became familiar to us. He had the ability to produce anæsthesia in many parts of his body, and stick hatpins through his tongue and cheeks without pain; he could go into a deep trance in which his body became rigid and cold; and I put his head on one chair and his heels on another, and stood in the middle, as if he were a two-inch plank. We have a motion picture film, showing a 150-pound rock being broken with a sledge-hammer on his abdomen while he lay in this trance. The vital faculties were so far suspended in this trance that he could be shut up in an airtight coffin and buried underground for several hours; nor was there any hocus-pocus about this—I know physicians who got the coffins and arranged for the tests and watched every detail; in Ventura, California, it was done in a ball park, and a game was played over the grave.

In our home he gave what appeared to be a demonstration of levitation without contact. I do not say that it really *was* levitation; I merely say that our friends who witnessed it—physicians, scientists, writers and their wives, fourteen persons in all—were unable even to suggest a normal method by which the event could have happened. There was no one present who could have been a confederate, and the psychic had been searched for apparatus; it was in our home, where he had no opportunity whatever for preparation. His wrists and ankles were firmly held by persons whom I know well; and there was sufficient light in the room so that I could see the outline of his figure, slumped in a chair. Under these circumstances a 34-pound table rose four feet into the air and moved slowly a distance of eight feet over my head.

We saw this; our friends saw it; yet, in my mind, and likewise in theirs, the worm of doubt would always creep in. There are so many ways to fool people; so many conjuring tricks—think of Houdini, for example! I was unwilling to publish what I had seen; yet, also, I was unwilling not to publish it—for think of the possible importance of faculties such as this, locked up in our minds! Here was my wife, ill, suffering pain; and these faculties might perhaps be used in healing. If by concentration and autosuggestion it was possible for the mind to control the body, and put a veto upon even a few of its disorders, certainly it was worth while for us to prove the fact. I could not escape the moral obligation to probe these matters.

This "psychic" claimed also to possess and demonstrate the power of telepathy, or mind-reading. He would go out of the room while one of as selected mentally some object in the room, not revealing the choice to any one else. The "psychic" would then come back, and tell us to stand behind him and concentrate our thoughts upon that object, and follow close behind him, thinking of it. He would wander about the room for a while, and in the end pick up the object, and do with it whatever we mentally "willed" him to do.

We saw him make this test not less than a hundred times, in California, New York, and Boston; he succeeded with it more than half the time. There was no contact, no word spoken, nothing that we could imagine as giving him a clue. Did we unconsciously make in our throats some faint pronunciation of words, and did the young man have a super-acuity of hearing? Again, you see, the worm of doubt, and we never could quite decide what we really believed about this performance. After puzzling over it for a year or more, my wife said: "There is only one way to be certain. I am going to learn to do these things *myself!*"

This young man, whom I will call Jan, was a peculiar person. Sometimes he would be open and frank, and again he would be mysterious and secretive. At one time he would agree to teach us all he knew, and again he would hold on to his arts, which he had had to go all the way to India to get. Was it that he considered these forces too dangerous for amateurs to play with? Or was it merely that he was considering his means of livelihood?

Jan was a hypnotist; and my wife had come to realize that all illness is more or less amenable to suggestion. She had had the idea of being hypnotized and given curative suggestions; but she did not know enough about this stranger, and was unwilling to trust him. After she got to know him better, her purposes changed. Here was a fund of knowledge which she craved, and she put her woman's wits to work to get it. She told him to go ahead and hypnotize her—and explained to me her purpose of trying to turn the tables on him. Jan fixed his eyes upon hers in the hypnotic stare, and made his magnetic passes; at the same time his patient stared back, and I sat and watched the strange duel of personalities.

An essential part of Jan's technique, as he had explained it, was in outstaring the patient and never blinking his eyes. Now suddenly he blinked; then he closed his eyes and kept them closed. "Do your eyes hurt?" asked his patient, in pretended innocence. "No," he replied. "Are you tired?" she asked. "No, thank you," said he. "What was I thinking?" she asked. "To hypnotize me," he replied, sleepily. But Craig wanted further proof, so she closed her eyes and willed that Jan should get up and go to the telephone. "Shall I go on treating you?" he asked. "Yes," said she. He hesitated a moment, then said, "Excuse me, I have to telephone to a friend!"

I am telling about these matters in the order of time, as they came to us. I am sorry that these stories of Jan come first, because they are the strangest, and the least capable of proof. In the hope of taking part of the onus from our shoulders, let me quote from a book by Charles Richet, a member of the Institute of Medicine in France, and a leading scientist; he is citing Pierre Janet, whose name is known wherever in the world the human mind is studied. The statement reads:

"P. Janet, a most eminent French psychiatrist, and one of the founders of the famous Salpetriere school of psychology in Paris, and a careful and sceptical observer, has verified that a patient of his, Leonie B., being put into hypnotic sleep by himself, or his brother (from whom Leonie in her hypnotic sleep was unable to distinguish him), could recognize *exactly* the substance that he placed in his mouth—sugar, salt, pepper. One day his brother, J. Janet, in an adjoining room, scorched his right arm above the wrist. Leonie, who could have known nothing about it normally, gave signs of real pain, and showed to P. Janet (who knew nothing of the occurrence), the exact place of the burn."

Or let me cite the late Professor Quackenbos, of Columbia University, who wrote many books on hypnotism as a therapeutic agency, and tells of numerous cases of the same kind. He himself would sometimes go involuntarily into hypnotic sleep with his patient, and so, sometimes, would the nurse. Frequently between the hypnotist and the subject comes what is called *rapport*, whereby each knows what is in the other's mind, and suggestions are taken without their being spoken. You may believe this, or refuse to believe it—that is your privilege. All I want to do is to make clear that my wife is claiming no special achievement, but merely repeating the standard experiences of the textbooks on this subject.

This *rapport* between Craig and her protégé was developed to such an extent that she could tell him what was in his mind, and what he had been doing; she told him many stories about himself, where he had been and what he had done at a certain hour. This was embarrassing to a young man who perhaps did not care to have his life so closely overseen; also, possibly, he was wounded in his *amour propre*, that a mere amateur—and a woman at that—should be coming into possession of his secret arts.

The trick depends upon a process of intense concentration, which will later be described in detail. After this concentration, Craig would give to her subconscious mind the suggestion, or command, that it should bring to her consciousness a vision of what Jan was doing. This giving an order to the subconscious mind is much the same sort of thing that you do when you seek to remember a name; whether you realize it or not, you order your subconscious mind to get that bit of information and bring it to you. Whatever came to Craig, she would write it out, and when next she met Jan, she would use her woman's wits to verify it without Jan's knowing what was happening. At times it would be very amusing—when he would find himself accused of some youthful misdemeanor which his preceptress was not supposed to know about. In his efforts to defend himself, he would fail entirely to realize the telepathic aspects of the matter.

V

PLEASE let me repeat, I am not telling here a set of fairy tales and fantasies; I am presenting a record of experiments, conducted in strict scientific fashion. All the results were set down day by day in writing. For an hour or two every day for the past three years my wife has been scribbling notes of her experiments, and there are eight boxes full in her study, enough to fill a big trunk. No statement in all the following rests upon our memories; everything is taken from memoranda now in my hands. Admitting that new facts can be learned about the mind, I do not see how any one can use more careful methods than we have done.

My wife "saw" Jan carrying a bouquet of flowers, wrapped in white paper, on the street, and she wrote this down. She later ascertained that at this hour Jan had carried flowers to a friend in a hospital in Los Angeles, and she telephoned this friend and verified the facts. On another occasion when Jan was in Santa Barbara, a hundred miles from our home, she "saw" him escorting a blonde girl in a blue dress from an auto to a hotel over a rainy pavement; she wrote this down, and later ascertained that it had actually been happening. The details were verified, not merely by Jan, but by another member of the party. I ought to add that in no case did my wife tell the other persons what she had "seen" until after these persons had told her what had happened. No chance was taken of their making up events to conform to her records. Always Craig kept her cold-blooded determination to know what was *real* in this field where so much is invented and imagined.

Again, she "saw" Jan preparing to commit suicide, dressed in a pair of yellow silk pajamas; then she "saw" him lying dead on the floor.

26

She was much disturbed—until Jan reminded her that he had been seven times publicly "buried" in Southern California before she met him. Several weeks later she learned that in one of these "burials" he had worn yellow silk pajamas. Jan had forgotten this, but Dr. Frank Sweet, of Long Beach, who had overseen the procedure, remembered the pajamas, and how they had been ruined by mud.

Craig saw a vision of a bride, at a time when Jan, in his room in a far part of the city, was awakening from sleep with a dream about a friend's wedding. On two occasions, while "concentrating," she got the impression that Jan and a friend of his had returned unexpectedly from Santa Barbara to Hollywood. In both cases she made careful record, and it turned out to be correct; I have a written statement of the two young men, confirming the second instance, and saying that it could not have been normally known to my wife.

I have also a detailed record—some twenty pages long—of a "clairvoyant" vision of Jan's movements about the city of Long Beach, including his parking of a car, carrying something over his arm, visiting a barber-shop and a flower-shop, and stopping and hesitating and then going on. The record includes a detailed description of the streets and their lay-out, a one-story white building, etc. Jan had been doing all this at approximately the time specified. He had carried his trousers to a tailor-shop, with a barber-shop directly opposite; he had stopped in front of a flower-shop and debated whether to buy some flowers; he had taken a letter to be copied by a typist, and had stopped on the street, hesitating as to whether to wait for this copying to be done. All these details he narrated to my wife *before* he knew what was in her written record.

Another curious experience: I took Jan to the home of Dr. John R. Haynes of Los Angeles, to give a demonstration of his mind-reading. Jan said he felt ill, and would not be successful. Only one or two of the tests succeeded. But meanwhile my wife was at home, concentrating, and ordering her subconscious mind to show her what Jan and I were doing. When I returned I found that she had written a detailed description of Dr. Haynes' home, including a correct ground plan of the entrance hall, stairs and drawing-room, and a description of the color and style of decorations, furniture,

27

lamps, vases, etc., in good part correct. Craig has never been in this house.

Jan goes into one of his deep states—a cataleptic trance, he calls it—in which his body is rigid and cold. He has the power to fix in advance the time when he will come out of the trance, and his subconscious mind apparently possesses the power to keep track of time—days, hours, minutes, even seconds. I have seen him amaze a group of scientists by coming out on the second, while they held stop-watches on him.

But now my wife thinks she will vary this procedure. Jan goes into the trance in our home and Craig sits and silently wills, "Your right leg will come out; you will lift it; you will put it down again. You will sit erect"—and so on. Without speaking a word, she can make him do whatever she pleases.

Another incident, quite a long one. I ask you to have patience with the details, promising that in the end you will see what it is all about. I am in the next room, and I hear Jan and my wife having one of their regular evening arguments, because he will not tell her how he does this or that; at one moment he insists that he has told her—and the next moment he insists that he does not know. My wife finally asks him to concentrate upon an object in the room, and she will see if she can "get" it. He selects the gas stove, in which a fire is burning; and Craig says, "I see a lot of little flames." Jan insists that is "no good," she didn't get the stove; which annoys her very much—she thinks he does not want to allow any success to a woman. He is a "continental male," something she makes fierce feminist war upon.

Craig is suffering from neuralgia in neck and shoulder, and Jan offers to treat her. He will use what he calls "magnetism"; he believes there is an emanation from his finger-tips, and so, with his two forefingers he lightly traces the course of the nerves of her neck and shoulder and arm. For ten or fifteen minutes his two fingers are tracing patterns in front of her.

Then it is time for him to go home, and he is unhappy, and she succeeds in drawing the explanation from him—he has to walk, and his shoes are tight and hurt him. He has to have them stretched, he tells her. She offers him a pair of my big tennis shoes to wear home, and then she scolds him because he has the fashionable notion that white canvas tennis shoes are not proper footwear for eleven o'clock in the evening. Finally he puts them on and departs; and my wife lies down and makes her mind a blank, and orders it to tell her what Jan is doing.

She has a pencil and paper, and presently she is writing words. They are foreign words, and she thinks they must be in Jan's native language; they come drifting through her mind for several minutes. Next day comes Jan for the daily lesson, and she shows him this record. He tells her that the words are not in his language, but German—which he knows, but never uses. My wife knows no German; except possibly sauerkraut and kindergarten. But here she has written a string of German and near-German words. I have the original sheet before me, and I give it as well as I can make out the scrawl: "ei einfinen ein-fe-en swenfenz fingen sweizzen czie ofen weizen ofen fingen sweinfen swei fingern efein boden fienzen meifen bogen feingen Bladen Meichen frefen eifein."

Some of this is nonsense; but there are a few German words in it, and others which are guesses at German words, such as might be made by a person hearing a strange language, and trying to set down what he hears. Part of the effort seems to be concentrated on getting one expression, "zwei Fingern"—two fingers! You remember the two fingers moving up and down over Craig's neck and shoulder! And "Ofen"—the argument about the stove! And "bladen"—to stretch shoes over a block of wood. Where these ideas came from seems plain enough. But where did the German come from—unless from the subconscious mind of Jan?

A further detail, especially curious. Jan gave my wife the meaning for the word "bladen": "to stretch shoes over a block of wood"; I have the memo which he wrote at the time. But looking up the word in the dictionaries, I do not find it, nor can I find any German who knows it. Apparently there is no such word; and this would clearly seem to indicate that my wife got her German from Jan. If so, it was by telepathy, for he spoke no word of it that evening.

It is the fashion among young ladies of the South to tease the men; and Craig found in this episode a basis for tormenting her psychic instructor. He had assured his patient that during the treatment he was sending her "curative thoughts." But what kind of telepathic healer was it who sent gas-stoves and shoe-blocks into a neuralgic shoulder? Jan, missing the humor, and trying to save his reputation, declared that he hated the German language so greatly, he did not even allow himself to think in it! Germany was associated in his mind with the most painful memories, and all that previous day he had been fighting depression caused by these memories. You see, in this blundering defense, a significant bit of evidence. Jan had really had the German language in his thoughts at the time Craig got them!

I have before me a letter from Jan to my wife, postmarked Santa Barbara, October 19, 1927. He says: "May these lovely Cosmos bring you such peace and contentment as they have brought me." He has cut a double slit in the paper, and inserted cosmos blossoms and violets. Prior to the receipt of this letter, my wife was making the record of a dream, and here is what she wrote down: "I dreamed Jan had a little basket of flowers, pink roses and violets, shaped like this." (A drawing.) "He lifted them up and said they were for me, but a girl near him took them and said, 'But I want them.'" When Jan came to see us again, my wife asked about the circumstance, and learned the following: a woman friend, who had given Jan the flowers, had accused him of meaning to send them to a girl; but he had answered that they were for "a middle-aged and distinguished lady."

I present here the basket of "pink roses and violets" which my wife drew, and then the spray of pink double cosmos and violets which met her eyes when she opened the young "psychic's" letter a day or two later. I explain that my wife's drawing (fig. 13) is partly written over by the words of her notes; while in Jan's letter the violets had to be at once traced in pencil, as they would not last.

My wife drew pencil marks around them and wrote the word "violet" in three places, to indicate what the marks meant. The cosmos flowers, pressed and dried, are still exactly as Jan stuck them into position and as they remained until I took them to be photographed (fig. 13).

30

Fig. 13

Fig. 13a

VI

As I have said, I hesitate to tell about incidents such as these. They are hard to believe, and the skeptic may say that my wife was hypnotized by Jan, and made to believe them. But it happens that Craig has been able to establish exactly the same *rapport* with her husband, who has never had anything to do with hypnosis, except to watch it a few times. A Socialist "muckraker," much wrapped up in his job, the husband sits and reads, or revises manuscript, while the wife works her white magic upon his mind. Suddenly his train of thought is broken by an exclamation; the wife has "willed" him to do such and so—and he has done it! Or maybe she has been asleep, and come out with the tail end of a dream, and has written down what appears to be a lot of rubbish—but turns out to be a reproduction of something the husband has been reading or writing at that very moment! Hear one or two instances of such events, all written down at the time.

Colonel Lindbergh has flown to France, but Craig does not know much about it, because she is not reading the papers, she is asking, "What is life?" A year passes, and in the mail I receive a monthly magazine, the "Lantern," published by Sacco-Vanzetti sympathizers in Boston. I open it, and find an article by a young radical, assailing Lindbergh because he does not follow in his father's footsteps; his father was a radical congressman, but now the son allows himself to be used by the army and navy people, and by the capitalist press, to distract the minds of the masses from social justice. So runs the charge; and before I am through reading it, my wife comes downstairs from a nap. "What are you reading?" she asks, and I answer: "Something about Lindbergh." Says my wife: "Here are my notes about a dream I just had." She hands me a sheet of paper, I have it before me now as I write, and I give it with misspelling and abbreviations exactly as she wrote it in a hurry, not anticipating that it would ever become public:

"'I do not believe that Lindberg flew across the ocean in order to take a ransome from a foreign gov as well as from his own. Nor in order to induce the nations of the earth to a war in the air.' Words which were in my mind as I awoke from nap on aft May 25."

I should add that my wife had had no opportunity to look at the Boston magazine, whether consciously or unconsciously. She tells me that Lindbergh had not been in her conscious mind for a long time, and she had no remotest idea that the radicals were attacking him.

Another instance: I am reading the latest "book of the month," which has just come in the mail, and to which my wife has paid no attention. She interrupts me with a question: "Are there any flowers in what you are reading?" I answer, "Yes," and she says: "I have been trying to concentrate, and I keep seeing flowers. I have drawn them." She hands me two drawings (figs. 14a, 14b):

Fig. 14a

Fig. 14b

The book was Mumford's "Herman Melville," and I was at page 346, a chapter entitled, "The Flowering Aloe." On this page are six lines from a poem called "The American Aloe on Exhibition." On the preceding page is a discussion of the habits of this plant. While my wife was making the left-hand drawing (fig. 14a), I had been reading page 344: "the red clover had blushed through the fields about their house"; and "he would return home with a handful of clover blossoms."

Of experiences like this there have been many. Important as the subject is, I find it a bother, because I am called upon to listen to long narratives of dreams and telepathy, while my mind is on Sacco and Vanzetti, or the Socialist presidential campaign, or whatever it is. Sometimes the messages from the subconscious are complicated and take patience to disentangle. Consider, for example, a little drawing (fig. 15)—one of nearly

33

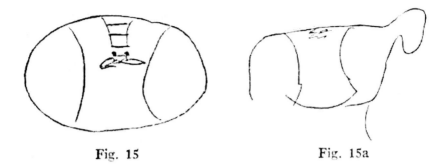

Fig. 15   Fig. 15a

three hundred which this long-suffering husband has made for his witch-wife to reproduce by telepathy: a football, you see, neatly laced up. In her drawing (fig. 15a) Craig gets the general effect perfectly, but she puts it on a calf. Her written comment was: "Belly-band on calf."

While Craig was making this particular experiment, her husband was reading a book; and now, wishing to solve the mystery, she asks, "What are you reading?" The husband replies, wearily: "DeKruif's 'Hunger Fighters,' page 283." "What does it deal with?" "It is a treatise on the feeding of cows." "Really?" says Craig. "Will you please write that down for me and sign it?"

But why did the cow become a calf? That, too, is something to be explained. Says Craig: "Do you remember what I used to tell you about old Mr. Bebb and his calves?" Yes, the husband knows the story of the half-crazy old Welshman, who thirty or forty years ago was the caretaker of the Kimbrough summer home on the Mississippi Sound. Old Mr. Bebb made his hobby the raising of calves by hand, and turning them into parlor pets. He would teach them to use his three fingers as a nursing bottle, and would make fancy embroidered belly-bands for them, and tie them up in these. So to the subconscious mind which was once little Mary Craig Kimbrough of Mississippi, the idea of a calf sewed up like a football is one of the most natural in the world.

Since my wife and I have no secrets from each other, it does not trouble me that she is able to see what I am doing. While I am away from home, she will "concentrate" upon me, and immediately afterwards write out what she "sees." On one occasion she

34

described to me a little red book which I had got in the mail at the office. By way of establishing just what kind of book she had "seen," she had gone to my bookcase and picked out a French dictionary—and it happened that I had just received the Italian dictionary of that same series, uniform in binding. On another occasion, while making a study of dream-material, she wrote out a dream about being lost in long and involved concrete corridors — while I was trying to find my way through the locker-rooms of a Y. M. C. A. basement, running into one blind passage after another, and being much annoyed by doors that wouldn't open.

Dreams, you understand, are products of subconscious activity, and to watch them is one method of proving telepathy. By practice Craig has learned to lie passive, immediately after awakening, and trace back a long train of dreams. Here is one of the results, a story worth telling in detail—save that I fear you will refuse to believe it after it is told.

On the afternoon of January 30, 1928, I was playing tennis on the courts of the Virginia Hotel, in Long Beach, California, and my wife was taking a nap. She did not know that I was playing tennis, and has no knowledge about the places where I play. She takes no interest in the game, regarding it as a foolish business which will some day cause her husband to drop dead of heart failure—and she declines to be present on the occasion. When I entered the house, she said: "I woke up with a long involved dream, and it seemed so absurd I didn't want to write it out, but I did so." Here are the opening sentences verbatim:

"Dreamed I was on a pier, watching a new kind of small, one or two seated sport-boat, a little water car into which a woman got and was shot by machinery from the pier out to the water, where she skidded around a minute or two and was drawn back to the pier. With us on the pier were my sister and child, and two young men in white with white caps. These appeared to be in charge of this new sport-boat. This boat is not really a boat. It is a sort of miniature car. I've never seen anything like it. Short, so that only one or two people could sit in it. An amusement thing, belonging to the pier. The two young men were intensely interested, and stood close together watching it out on the water," etc., etc.

Understand that this dream was not supposed to have anything to do with me. It was before Craig had come to realize the state of *rapport* with me; she had not been thinking about me, and when she told me about this dream, she had no thought that any part of it had come from my mind. But here is what I told her about my afternoon:

The Virginia Hotel courts are close to what is called "The Pike," and there is an amusement pier just across the way, and on it a so-called "Ferris wheel," with little cars exactly like the description, which go up into the air with people in them. That afternoon it happened that the tennis courts were crowded, so my partner and I waited out a set or two. We sat on a bench, in white tennis suits and hats, and watched this wheel, and the cars which went up in the air, and at a certain point took a slide on long rods, which made them "skid around," and caused the women in them to scream with excitement. Underneath the pier was the ocean, plainly visible along with the little cars.

I should also mention the case of our friend, Mrs. Kate Crane-Gartz, with whom there is a *rapport* which my wife does not tell her about. My wife will say to me, "Mrs. Gartz is going to phone," and in a minute or two the phone will ring. She will say, "Mrs. Gartz is coming. She wants me to go to Los Angeles with her." Of course, a good deal of guessing might be possible, in the case of two intimate friends. But consider such guessing as this: My wife had a dream of an earthquake and wrote it down. Soon thereafter occurred this conversation with Mrs. Gartz. I heard it, and my wife recorded it immediately afterwards, and I quote her written record:

"Mrs. Gartz dreamed of earthquake. 'Wasn't it queer that I dreamed of swaying slowly from side to side.'

"'I dreamed the same,' I said. 'But I was in a high building.'"

"'So was I,' she replied."

Craig calls attention to the word "slowly," as both she and Mrs. Gartz commented on this. They didn't believe that an earthquake would behave that way; but I pointed out that it would happen just so with a steel-frame building.

VII

I COME now to a less fantastic and more convincing series of experiments; those made with the husband of my wife's younger sister, Robert L. Irwin. Eight years ago the doctors gave Bob only a few months to live, on account of tuberculosis. Needless to say, he has much time on his hands, waiting for the doctors' clairvoyance to be verified. He proved to be a good "subject"—the best of all in the tests with Jan. One day in our home, a series of five tests were made, with Bob holding an object in mind, while sitting several feet away from Jan. The latter found the object, and made the correct disposition of it, as willed by Bob, in four out of the five trials. This included such unlikely things as picking up a striped blanket and wrapping it about my shoulders.

Bob and Craig made the arrangement that at a certain hour each day, Bob, in his home in Pasadena, was to take pencil and paper and make a drawing of an object, and sit and concentrate his mind upon that drawing. At the same hour Craig, in our home in Long Beach, forty miles away, was to go into her state of "concentration," and give orders to her subconscious mind to find out what was in Bob's mind. The drawings were to be dated, and filed, and when the two of them met, they would compare the results, in the presence of myself and Bob's wife. If there should turn out to be a correspondence between the drawings, greater than could be attributed to chance, it would be evidence of telepathy, as good as any that could be imagined or desired.

The results were such as to make me glad that it was another person than myself, so as to afford a disinterested witness to these matters, so difficult of belief. I repeat that Bob is a young American business man, priding himself on having no "crank" ideas; he has had a Socialist brother-in-law for ten years or more without being in the slightest degree affected in manners, morals, or convictions. Here is his first drawing, done on a half sheet of green paper. The word "CHAIR" underneath, and the date, were written by Bob, while the words "drawn by Bob Irwin" were added for purposes of record by Craig (fig. 16):

Fig. 16

And now for Craig's results. I give her report verbatim, with the two drawings which are part of her text:

"At 10 o'clock or a little before, while sewing (without effort) I saw Bob take something from black sideboard—think it was the glass candlestick. At 11:15 (I concentrate now) I saw Bob sitting at dining room table—a dish or some small object in front of him (on N. E. corner table). I try to see the object on table—see white something at last. I can't decide what it is so I concentrate on seeing his drawing on a green paper as it is about 11:20 now and I think he has made his drawing. I try hard to see what he has drawn—try to see a paper with a drawing on it, and see a straight chair. Am not sure of second drawing. It does not seem to be on his paper. It may his bed-foot. I distinctly see a chair like 1st on his paper." (fig. 16a):

Fig. 16a

When Bob and my wife discussed the above test, she learned that he had sat at the northeast corner of the table, trying to decide what to draw, and facing the sideboard on which were silver candlesticks. Later he went to his bedroom and lay down, gazing through the foot of his bed at the chair which he had taken as his model for the drawing. The bed has white bars running vertically, as in my wife's second drawing. The chair, like Bob's drawing, has the strips of wood supporting the back running crossways, and this feature is reproduced in Craig's first drawing. Her report goes on to add that she sees a star and some straight lines, which she draws; they are horizontal parallel lines, as in the back of the chair. The back of the chair Bob had looked at had a carved star upon it.

The second attempt was the next day, and Bob drew his watch (fig. 17). Craig first drew a chair, and then wrote, "But do not feel it is correct." Then she drew the following (fig. 17a):

The comment was: "I see this picture. Later I think it is not flower but wire (metal, shining). The 'petals' are not petals but wire, and should

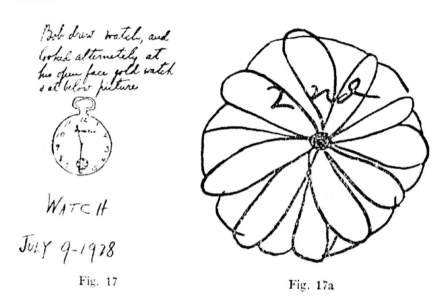

Fig. 17

Fig. 17a

be *uniform*. This is hasty drawing so not exact as seen. What I mean is, I try to see Bob's drawing and not what he drew from. So I see no flower but shape of one on paper. Then decide it is of wire, but this may be merely because I see drawing, which would have no flower color. However, I see it shining as if it is metal. Later a glass circle." Drawings then show an ellipse, and then a drinking glass and a glass pitcher. It is interesting to note that Bob had in front of him a glass bowl with gold-fish.

The next day Bob drew a pair of scissors (fig. 18):

Original of above drawing

SCISSORS
JULY 10-1928

Fig. 18

The drawings of Craig follow without comment (figs. 18a, 18b):

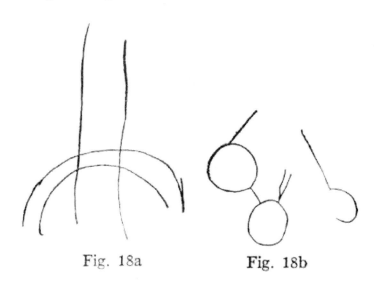

Fig. 18a   Fig. 18b

Three days later Bob drew the table fork, which has already been reproduced (fig. 1), and Craig made the report which has been given in facsimile (fig. 1a): "See a table fork. Nothing else."

One more test between Bob and Craig, the most sensational of all. It is quite a story, and I have to ask your pardon for the medical details involved. So much vital knowledge hangs upon these tests that I have asked my brother-in-law to forget his personal feelings. The reader will please consider himself a medical student or hospital nurse for the moment.

The test occurred July 11, 1928. My wife made her drawing, and then told me about the matter at once. Also she wrote out all the details and the record is now before me. She saw a feather, then a flower spray, and then she heard a scream. Her first thought in case of illness or danger is her aged parents, and she took it for her mother's voice, and this so excited her that she lost interest in the experiment. But soon she concentrated again, and drew a series of concentric circles, with a heavy black spot in the center. Then she saw another and much larger spot, and this began to spread and cover the sheet of paper. At the same time came a feeling of intense depression, and Craig decided that the black spot was blood, and that Bob had had a hemorrhage. Here is her drawing (fig. 19a)

Fig. 19a

Two or three days later Bob's wife drove him to our home, and in the presence of all

42

four of us he produced the drawing he had made. He had taken a compass and drawn a large circle; making, of course, a hole in the center of the paper. "Is that all you thought of during the time?" asked my wife. "No," said Bob, "but I'd hate to have you get the rest of it." "What was it?" "Well, I discovered that I had a hemorrhoid, and couldn't put my mind on anything else but the thought, 'My God, my lungs—my kidneys—and now this!'"

A hemorrhoid is, of course, apt to be accompanied by a hemorrhage; and it seems clear that my wife got the mood of depression of her brother-in-law, his thoughts of blood and bodily breakdown, as well as the circle and the hole in the paper. There is another detail which does not appear in the written record, but is fixed in my memory. My wife said: "I wanted to draw a little hill." Upon hearing that, I called up a physician friend who is interested in these tests, and asked him what a drawing of a hemorrhoid would look like, and he agreed that "a little hill' was about as near as one could come. I hope you will note that this particular drawing test is supported by the testimony of four different persons, my wife, her sister, the sister's husband, and myself. I do not see how there could possibly be more conclusive evidence of telepathic influence—unless you suspect all four of us of a series of stupid and senseless falsehoods. Let me repeat that Bob and his wife have read this manuscript and certified to its correctness so far as concerns them. The comment written by my wife reads: "All this dark like a stain—feel it is blood; that Bob is ill—more than usual."

VIII

THE experiments just described were all that were done with Bob, because he found them a strain. Craig asked me to make some drawings for her, and I did so, sitting in the next room, some thirty feet away, but always behind a closed door. Thus you may verify my assertion that the telepathic energy, whatever it may be, knows no difference between thirty feet and forty miles. The results with Bob and with myself were about the same.

The first drawings made with me are those which have already been given (fig. 2, 2a), but I give them again for the sake of convenience. I explain that in these particular drawings the lines have been traced over in heavier pencil; the reason being that Craig wanted a carbon copy, and went over the lines in order to make it. This had the effect of making them heavier than they originally were, and it made the whirly lines in Craig's first drawing more numerous than they should be. She did this in the case of two or three of the early drawings, wishing to send a report to a friend. I pointed out to her how this would weaken their value as evidence, so she never did it again.

After my wife and I had compared the above drawings, she wrote a note to the effect that just before starting to concentrate, she had been looking at her drawing of many concentric circles, which she had made in a test with Bob the previous day (fig. 19a). So her first vision was of a whirl of circles. This turned sideways, and then took the shape of an arrowhead, and then of a letter A, and finally evolved into a complete star. As the agent in this test, I wish to repeat that I made my drawing in my study with the door closed, that I kept it before my eyes the entire time, and that the door stayed closed until Craig called that she was through.

I do not find it easy to concentrate on a drawing, because my active mind wanders off to side issues. If I draw a lighted cigarette, I immediately think of the odious advertising now appearing in the papers; or I think: "Will Craig get this right, and what does it mean, and will the world accept evidence on this subject from me?"—and so on. Several times my wife has "got" such thoughts, and so we took to noting them on the record. On July 29, I drew a cigarette, with two little curls for smoke, each running off like a string of the letter "eeeee," written by hand. Underneath I wrote as follows: "My thought: 'cigarette with curls of smoke.' I said to myself these words: 'she got the curls but not the cigarette.'"

This would appear to be telepathy coming from Craig to me, for her drawing was found to contain a lot of different curves—a curly capital S, several other half circles twisted together, and three???

one inside the other. She added the following words: "I can't draw it, but curls of some sort."

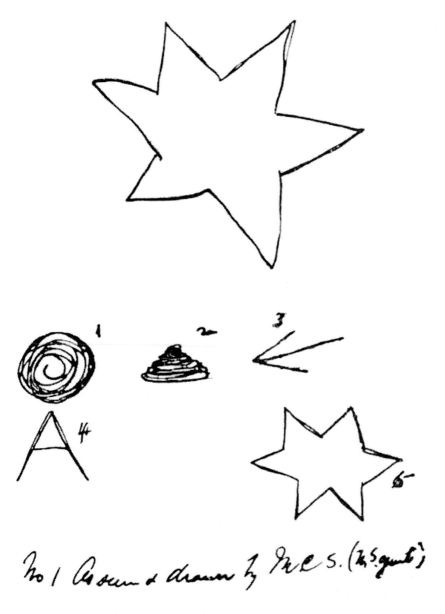

No 1 As seen & drawn by M.C.S. (th. Sgunti)

Again, here is a work of art from my facile pen, dated July 21, and having underneath my notation: "Concentrated on bald head" (fig. 20)

My wife's note was: "Saw Upton's face." Then she drew a line through the words, and wrote the following explanation: "Saw two

45

half circles. Then they came together making full circle. But I felt uncertain as to whether they belonged together or not. Then suddenly saw Upton's profile float across vision."

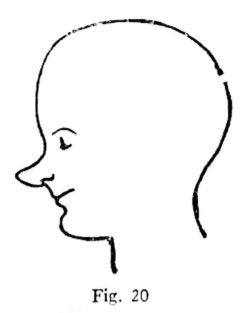

Fig. 20

July 20, I drew a three-pronged fork, and made the note that I was not sure if it was a hay-fork or an oyster-fork, and decided it was the latter, whereupon my mind went off to "society" people and their many kinds of forks. Craig wrote: "I thought it was an animal's head with horns, and the head was on a long stick—a trophy mounted like this"—and she drew a two-pronged fork.

July 17 I drew a large round stone with a smaller stone on top: at least so I thought, and then decided they were two eggs. Craig drew two almost tangent circles, and wrote: "I see two round things, not one inside the other, as in Bob's drawing of circles. Then the above vanished and I saw as below"—and she drew four little oblongs, tangent, which might be a cluster of fish-eggs or fly-eggs.

July 20 I drew two heavy straight lines making a capital letter T, and Craig drew a complete cross or square X, which is, of course, the T with vertical arm prolonged. July 14 I drew a sort of jack-lantern. It is on next page (fig. 21). I looked at this drawing and thought of the eyes of M.C.S., and said mentally, "I should have

46

Fig. 21

drawn the curves over eyes." Afterwards I told Craig about this, and she noted it down on the drawing. On the reverse side of the sheet

she added the following: "I told U. it was shaped like a half moon with something in center—I supposed it must be a star, though I did not see it as star but as indistinct marks." Her drawing follows, turned upside down for greater convenience (<u>fig. 21a</u>):

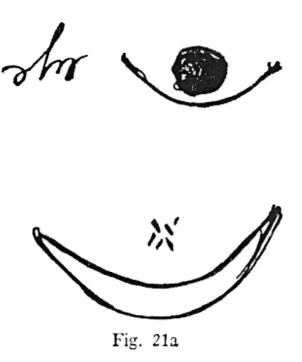

Fig. 21a

IX

A NEW method of experiment invented itself by accident; and makes perhaps the strangest story yet. There came a letter from a clergyman in South Africa, saying that he was sending me a copy of his wife's novel dealing with South African life. I get many letters from strangers, and answer politely, and as a rule forget them quickly. Some time afterwards came two volumes, entitled, "Patricia, by Marcus Romondt," and I did not associate them with the clergyman's letter. I glanced at the preface, and saw that the work had something to do with the religious cults of the South African natives. I didn't read more than twenty lines—just enough to classify the book as belonging in Craig's department. Everything having to do with philosophy, psychology, religion and medicine is first read by her, and then fed back to me in her eager discourses. I took the volumes home and laid them on her table, saying, "This may interest you." The remark attracted no special attention, for the reason that I bring her a book, or a magazine, or some clippings at least once a day. She did not touch these volumes, nor even glance at the title while I was in the room.

I went into the kitchen to get some lunch, and when it was ready I called, "Are you going to eat?" "Let me alone," she said, "I am writing a story." That also is a common experience. I ate my lunch in silence, and then came into the living room again, and there was Craig, absorbed in writing. Some time later she came to me, exclaiming, "Oh, I have had the most marvelous idea for a story! Something just flashed over me, something absolutely novel—I never heard anything like it. I have a whole synopsis. Do you want to hear it?" "No," I said, "you had better go and eat"—for it is my job to try to keep her body on earth. "I can't eat now," she said, "I am too excited. I'll read a while and get quiet." So she went to her couch, and there was a minute or two of silence, and then an exclamation: "Come here!"

Craig had picked up one of the two volumes from South Africa, and was staring at it. "Look at this! " she said. "Look what I opened to!" I looked at a page in the middle of the book—she has the devilish habit of reading a book that way—and in the center of the page, in capital letters, I read the words: "THE BLACK MAGICIAN." "What about it?" I said. "Did you ever hear of that idea?" asked Craig. I

48

answered that I had, and she said, "Well, I never did. I thought it was my own. It is the theme of the 'story' I have just been writing. I have made a synopsis of a whole chapter in this book, and without ever having touched it!"

So Craig had a new set of experiments to try all by herself, without bothering her busy husband. She would go to one of my bookcases, with which she had hitherto had nothing to do, since her own books are kept in her own place. With her back to the bookcase, she would draw a book, and take it to her couch and lie down, placing the book upon her solar plexus, and taking every precaution to make sure that it never came into her line of vision. Most of the books, being new, were in their paper jackets, so there was no lettering that could be felt with her fingers. This, you note, is not a test of telepathy, for no human mind knew what particular book Craig's hand had fallen upon. If she could tell anything about the contents of that book, it would appear to be clairvoyance, or what is known as "psychometry."

My books are oddly varied in character. There are new novels, and works of history, biography, travel and economics. In addition, there are what I call "crank books"; the queerly assorted volumes which are destined by donors all over the world to convert me to vegetarianism, antivivisection, anarchism, Mormonism, Mohammedanism, infanticide, the abolition of money, or the doctrine that alopecia is caused by onanism. Believe me, the person who sets out to guess the contents of the books that come to me in the course of a month has his or her hands full!

But Craig was able to do it. She did it on so many occasions that she would sit and stare at me and exclaim, "Now what do you make of *that?*" She would insist that I sit and watch the process, so as to be able to state that she never had the book in her line of vision. In my presence she picked out a volume, and, keeping it hidden from both of us, she said, "I see a blue cover, with a rising sun and a bare landscape." It happened to be a volume circulated by the followers of "Pastor Russell," and as the preface tells me that 1,405,000 have been sold, it may be that you too have it in your library. The title is "Deliverance," by J. F. Rutherford, and it has a blue cloth cover, with a gold design of a sun rising behind a mass of clouds and a globe.

On another occasion Craig wrote: "One big eye, with nothing else distinct—then lines or spikes came around it, or maybe these project from the head like stiff long hairs, or eye-lashes. Can't tell what kind of head—but feel it must be a tropical something, tho the eye looks human," etc. The book was "Mr. Blettsworthy on Rampole Island," by H. G. Wells, and in this book is a chapter headed, "The Friendly Eye," with the following sentences: "I became aware that an Eye observed me continually. . . . It was a reddish brown eye. It looked out from a system of bandages that also projected a huge shock of brown hair upward and a great chestnut beard . . . the eye watched me with the illuminating but expressionless detachment of a head-lamp. . . . Polyphemus, for that was my private name for the man."

A long string of such surprises! Craig picked up a book and wrote: "Black wings—a vampire flying by night." The title of the book was "The Devil's Jest." She picked up one and wrote: "A Negro's head with a light around it." It is a German volume, called "Africa Singt," and has a big startling design exactly as described. She picked up a book by Leon Trotsky, and wrote the word "Checkro"—which may not sound like Russian to Trotsky, but does to Craig! And a book with Mussolini on the cover, wearing a black coat and feeding a lion; she got the shape of the Duce's figure, only she labeled him "Black Bird." And here is a part of the jacket design of "wings" on the "Literary Guild" books—and below is what Craig made of it. She added the comment: "Motion—the thing is traveling, point first" (<u>fig. 22, 22a</u>):

Fig. 22

Fig. 22a

Another volume was described as follows: "A pale blue book. Lonely prairie country, stretch of flat land against sky, and outlined against it a procession of people. Had feeling of moving—wheeled vehicle which seemed to be baby-carriage. This was strange, because country was covered with snow." Upon examination, the book proved to be bound in mottled pale blue boards, title, "I'm Scairt," with subtitle, "Childhood Days on the Prairies." On the first page of the preface occurs the following: "It was in those days that a company of Swedes left their beloved homeland in the far North and came to make a home for themselves and their children on the Kansas prairie."

Finally, I have obtained the publisher's consent to reproduce the jacket design of a recent book, so that I may put Craig's telepathy alongside it, and give you a laugh or two. Observe the jolly little tourists, and what they have turned into! And then the efforts of Craig's subconscious mind at French. They taught it to her in a "finishing school" on Fifth Avenue, and you can see that it was finished before it began (fig. 23, 23a):

france is full
of frenchmen

by lewis galantière

payson & clarke ltd

Fig. 23

Fig. 23a

Yet another form of experiment invented itself under the pressure of necessity. Impossible to have such a witch-wife without trying to put her to use!

I have the habit of working out a chapter of a new book in my head, and writing down a few notes on a scrap of paper, and sticking it away in any place that is handy; then, next day, or whenever I am ready for work, it is gone, and there is the devil to pay. I wander about the house for an hour or two, trying to imagine where I can have put that scrap of paper, and reluctant to do the work all over again. On one occasion I searched every pocket, my desk, the trash-baskets, and then, deciding that I had dropped it outdoors, where I work with my typewriter, I figured the direction of the wind, and picked up all the scraps of paper I saw decorating the landscape of our beach home. Then I decided it must be in a manuscript which I had given to a friend in Los Angeles, and I was about to phone to that friend, when Craig asked what the trouble was, and said, "Come, let's make an experiment. Lie down here, and describe the paper to me."

I told her, a sheet off a little pad, written on both sides, and folded once. She took my hand, and went into her state of concentration, and said, "It is in the pocket of a gray coat." I answered, "Impossible; I have searched every coat in the house half a dozen times." She said, "It is in a pocket, and I will get it." She got up off the couch, and went to a gray coat of mine, and in a pocket I had somehow overlooked, there was the paper! Let me add that Craig had had nothing to do with my clothing in the interim, and had never seen the paper, nor heard of it until I began roaming about the house, grumbling and fussing. Neither of us know of any "normal" way by which her subconscious mind could have got this information.

My secretary lost two screw-caps of the office typewriter, and I said to my wife, "I will bring him over, and you see if you can tell him where to look." But my wife was ill, and did not want to meet any one, so she said, "I will see if I can get it through you." Be it understood, Craig has not been to the office in a year, and has met my secretary only casually. She said, "I see him standing up at his typewriting." That is an unusual thing for a typist to do, but it happened to be true. Said Craig: "He has put the screw-caps on something high. They are in the south room, above the level of any table or desk." I went to the phone to ask my secretary, and learned that he had just found the screws, which he had put on top of a window-sash in the south room.

The third incident requires the statement that, a few months back, while my wife was away, our home had been loaned to friends, and I had camped at the little house, which I was using as an office. Some medical apparatus had been left there; at least I had a vague impression that I had had it there, and I said, "I'll go and look." Said Craig: "Let's try an experiment." She took my hand, and told me to make my mind a blank, and presently she said, "I see it under the kitchen sink." I went over to the office, and found the object, not under the sink, but under the north end of the bathtub. I took it back to the house, and before I spoke a word, my wife said: "I tried to get you on the phone. I concentrated again, and saw the thing and wrote it out." She gave me a slip of paper, from which I copy: "Down under something, wrapped in. paper—on N. side of room—under laundry tub on floor or under bath tub on floor in N. corner."

You may say, of course, if you are an incurable skeptic: "The man's wife had been over to the office and seen the object; she had been searching his pockets, and had seen the paper." Craig is positive that she did nothing of the sort; but of course it is conceivable that she may have done it and then forgotten it. Therefore, I pass on to a different and more acceptable kind of evidence—a set of drawing tests, in which I watched and checked every step of the proceedings at my wife's insistence. Here again I am a co-equal witness with her, and the skeptic has no alternative but to say that the two of us have contrived this elaborate hoax, making nearly three hundred drawings with fake reproductions, in order to get notoriety, or to sell a few books. I really hope nobody will say that is possible. Very certainly I could sell more books with less trouble by writing what the public wants; and if I were a dishonest man, I should not have waited until the age of fifty-one to begin such a career.

X

CONCERNING these drawings, there are preliminary explanations to be made. They were done hastily, by two busy people. Neither is a trained artist, and our ability to convey what we wish is limited. When I start on a giraffe, I manage to produce a pretty good neck, but when I get to the body, I am disturbed to note it turning into a sheep or a donkey. When I draw a monkey climbing a tree, and Craig says, "Buffalo or lion, tiger—wild animal"—I have to admit that may be so; likewise when my limb of a tree is called a "trumpet," or when Craig's "wild animal" resembles a chorus girl's legs. I will let you see those particular drawings. Figure 24 is mine, while 24a and 24b are my wife's.

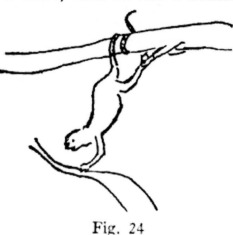

Fig. 24

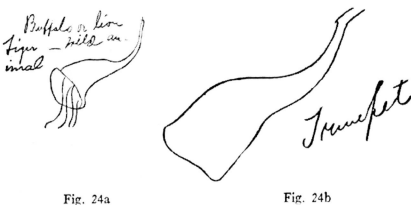

Fig. 24a   Fig. 24b

Again, I draw a volcano in eruption, and my wife calls it a black beetle, which hardly sounds like a triumphant success; but study the drawings, and you see that my black smoke happens to be the shape of a beetle, while the two sides of the volcano serve very well for the long feelers of an insect (fig. 25, 25a):

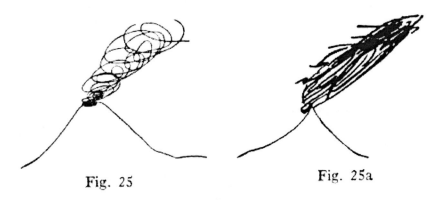

Fig. 25   Fig. 25a

The tests began with four series of drawings, 38 in all, made by my secretary. Following these were 31 series drawn by myself, comprising 252 separate drawings. Each drawing would be wrapped in an extra sheet of paper, and sealed in a separate envelope, and the envelopes handed to my wife when she was ready for the tests. She would put them on the table by her couch, and lie down, putting the first envelope, unopened, over her solar plexus, covered by her hand. Her head would be lying back on a pillow, eyes closed, and head at such an angle that nothing but the ceiling could be seen if the eyes were open. A dim light to avoid

55

sense stimulation; enough light to see everything plainly. When she had what she judged was the right image, she would take a pad and pencil and make the drawing or write the description of what she "saw." Then she would open the envelope and compare the two drawings, and number both for identification.

This recording was, of course, an interruption of her passive state, and made the task difficult. In a few cases she repeated a number or forgot the number, and this leaves a chance for confusion. I have done my best to clear up all such uncertainties, but there is a margin of error of one or two per cent to be noted. This is too small to affect the results, but is mentioned in the interest of exactness.

Since I found the sealing of envelopes tiresome, and Craig found the opening of them more so, we decided half way through the tests to abandon the sealing, and later we abandoned the envelopes altogether. We reasoned that acceptance of the evidence rests upon our good faith anyhow, and all that any sensible reader can ask is that Craig makes sure of never letting a drawing get within her range of vision. She was doing this laborious work to get knowledge for herself, and she certainly made sure that she was not wasting her own time.

At present the practice is this: I make her a set of six or eight drawings on little sheets of pad paper, and lay them face down on her table, with a clean sheet of paper over them. She lies down, and with her head lying back on the pillow and her eyes closed, she reaches for one of the drawings, and slides it over and onto her body, covered by her hand. It is always out of her range of vision, even if the drawing were turned towards her eyes, which it never is.

For the comfort of the suspicious, let me add that the relaxing of the conditions caused no change in the averages. In the first four series, drawn by my secretary, and sealed by him in envelopes, there were only five complete failures in thirty-eight tests, which is thirteen per cent; whereas in the 252 drawings made by me there have been 65 outright failures, which is nearly twice as large a percentage. Series number six, which was carefully sealed up, produced four complete successes, five partial successes, and no failures; whereas series twenty-one, which was not put in envelopes at all, produced no complete successes, three partial successes, and six failures. Perhaps I should explain that by a "series" I mean simply a group of drawings which were done at one time. It is my custom to make from six to a dozen and when Craig has finished with them, they are put into an envelope and filed away.

I will add that Craig again and again begged me to sit and watch her work, so that I might be able to add my testimony to hers; I did so, watching tests both with envelopes and without, and assure you she left no loophole for self-deception. There was plenty of light to see by, and some of the most startling successes were produced under my eyes. I will add that no one could take this matter with more seriousness than my wife. She is the most honorable person I know, and she has worked on these experiments with rigid conscientiousness.

XI

I SHALL give a number of the successful drawings, and some of the partial successes, but none of the failures, for these obviously are merely waste. When I draw a cow, and my wife draws a star or a fish or a horseshoe, all you want is the word "Failure," and then you want to know the percentage of failures, so that you can figure the probabilities. Failures prove nothing that you do not already believe; if your ideas are to be changed, it is successes that will change them.

I begin with series three, because of the interesting circumstances under which it was made. Late in the afternoon I phoned my secretary to make a dozen drawings; and then, after dark, Craig and I decided to drive to Pasadena, and on the way I stopped at the office and got the twelve sealed envelopes which had been laid on my desk. I picked them up in a hurry and slipped them into a pocket, and a minute or two later I put them on the seat beside me in the car.

After we had started, I said, "Why don't you try some of the drawings on the way?" We were passing through the Signal Hill oil-field, amid thunder of machinery and hiss of steam and flashing of headlights of cars and trucks. "It will be interesting to see if I can concentrate in such circumstances," said Craig, and took one envelope and held it against her body in the darkness, while I went on with my job of driving. After a few minutes Craig said, "I see something long and oblong, like a stand." She got a pad and pencil from a pocket of the car, and switched on the ceiling light, and made a drawing, and then opened the envelope. Here are the pictures; I call it a partial success (fig. 26, 26a):

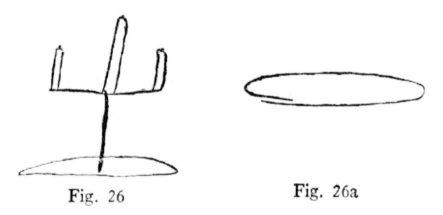

Fig. 26   Fig. 26a

Here is the next pair, done on the same drive to Pasadena (figs. 27, 27a):

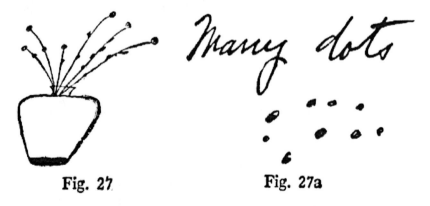

Fig. 27   Fig. 27a

Then came a drawing of an automobile. Considering the attendant circumstances, it was surely not surprising that Craig should report it as "a big light in the end of a tube or horn." There were many such lights in her eyes.

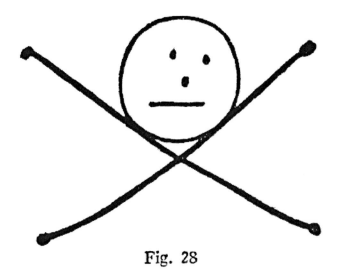

Fig. 28

Then a fourth envelope: she said, "I see a little animal or bug with legs, and the legs sticking out in bug effect." When she looked into the envelope, she was so excited that she tried to get me to look— at forty miles an hour on a highway at night! Here is the drawing, meant to be a skull and cross-bones, but so done that a "bug with legs" is really a fair description of it (fig. 28):

After we arrived at our destination, my wife did some more of the drawings, and got partial successes. On this telephone the comment was:

"Goblet with another one floating near or above it inverted" (figs. 29, 29a):

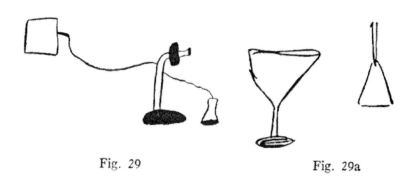

Fig. 29   Fig. 29a

And then this arrow (figs. 30, 30a):

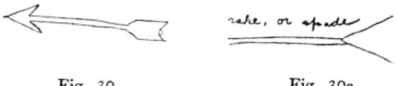

Fig. 30   Fig. 30a

Concerning the above my wife wrote: "See something that suggests a garden tool—a lawn rake, or spade." And for the next one (fig. 31) she wrote: "A pully-bone"—which is Mississippi "darky" talk for a wish-bone of a chicken. I don't know whether it means a bone that you pull, or whether it is Creole for "poulet." Here is what my secretary had drawn (fig. 31):

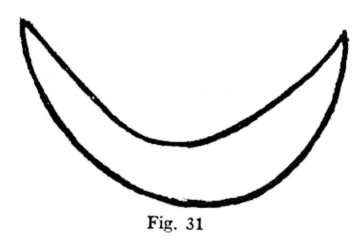

Fig. 31

I had asked my secretary at the outset to make simple geometrical designs, letters and figures, thinking that these would be easier to recognize and reproduce. But they brought only partial successes; Craig would get elements of the drawing, but would not know how to put them together. There were seven in the first series, and there is some element right in every one. An oblong was drawn exactly, and then two fragments of oblongs added to it. A capital M in script had the first stroke done exactly, with the curl. A capital E in script was done with the curls left out.

And the same with the second series. Here is a square—but you see that the two halves of it are wandering about (fig. 32, 32a):

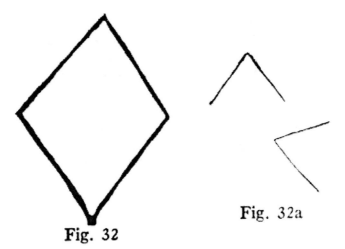

Fig. 32a

Fig. 32

And here is a letter Y, but by telepathy it has been turned from script into print (fig. 33, 33a):

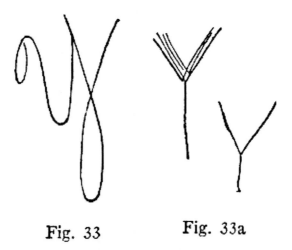

Fig. 33   Fig. 33a

A quite different story began when my secretary allowed his imagination a little play. He knows that my wife lives in part on milk, and he knows that she is particular about the quality, because he has to handle the bills. So he has a little fun with her, and you

61

see that immediately she gets, not the form, but the color and feeling of it (figs. 34, 34a):

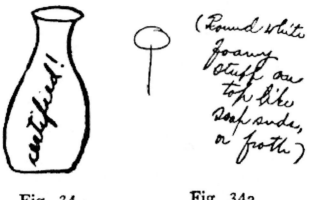

Fig. 34   Fig. 34a

The comment reads: "Round white foamy stuff on top like soap suds or froth." As she drinks her milk sour and whipped, you see that its foaminess is a prominent feature.

Then comes an oil derrick. We live in the midst of these unsightly objects, and are liable to be turned out of house and home by drilling nearby; moreover, I have written a book called "Oil! " and the exclamation mark at the end has been justified by the effect of it on our lives. My wife made a figure five with long lines going out, and wrote: "I don't know why the five should have such a thing as an appendage, but the appendage was most vivid, so there it is" (figs. 35, 35a):

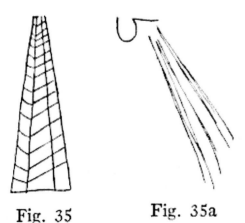

Fig. 35   Fig. 35a

After she had opened the envelope and seen the original drawing, the problem became, not why a figure five should have an appendage, but why an oil derrick should have a figure five. Craig puzzled over this, and then lay down and told her subconscious mind to bring her the answer. What came was this: the German version of my book, called "Petroleum," has three oil derricks on the front, and a huge dollar sign on the back of the cover, and this was what Craig had really "seen." She had looked at this book when it arrived, a year or more back, and it had been filed away in her memory. Of course this may not be the correct explanation, but it is the one which her mind brought to her.

XII

THESE drawing tests afford a basis for psychoanalysis, and it is interesting to note some of the facts thus brought up from the childhood of my wife. For example, fires! She was raised in the "black belt," where there are nine Negroes to one white, and the former are still close to Africa. When Craig was a girl, a nurse in the family, having been discharged, set fire to the home while the adults were away, and the children asleep. Another servant, jealous of an unfaithful husband, put her two babies into a barrel full of feathers and burned them alive. Other fires occurred; so now, in her home, Craig keeps an uneasy eye out for greasy rags, or overheated stoves, or whatever else her fears suggest. When in these drawing tests there has been anything indicating fire or smoke, she has "got" it, with only one or two failures out of more than a dozen cases. Sometimes she "got" the fire or smoke without the object; sometimes she supplied fire or smoke to an object which might properly have it—a pipe, for example. The results are so curious that I assemble them together—a series of fire-alarms, as it were.

You recall the fact that in one of the early drawing tests—those in which, instead of giving the drawings to my wife, I sat in my study and concentrated upon them—I drew a lighted cigarette, and thought of the curls of smoke. Craig filled up her drawing with curves, and wrote: "I can't draw it, but curls of some sort." At this time the convention that "curls" stood for smoke had not been established. But now, in the series drawn by my secretary, appeared a little house with smoking chimney, and you will see that my wife got the smoke better than the house (figs. 36, 36a):

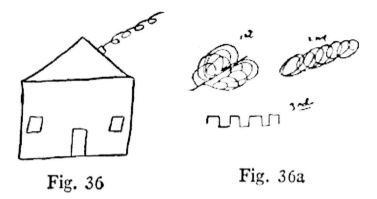

Fig. 36

Fig. 36a

This apparently established in her mind the association of curls with smoke. So when, in series six, I drew a pipe with smoke-curls, my wife first drew an ellipse, and then wrote: "Now it begins to spin, round and round, and is attached to a stick." She then drew (figs. 37, 37a):

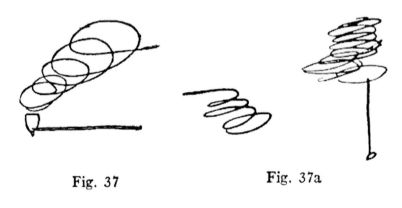

Fig. 37

Fig. 37a

In series eight I drew a sky-rocket going up. My first impulse had been to draw a bursting rocket, with a shower of stars, but I realized that would be difficult, so I drew this instead (fig. 38):

My wife apparently took my first thought, rather than my drawing. Anyhow, she made half a dozen sketches of whirligigs and light (figs. 38a, 38b, 38c):

Fig. 38

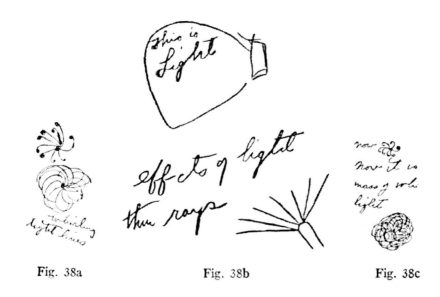

Fig. 38a   Fig. 38b   Fig. 38c

And here in series twenty-two is a burning lamp (figs. 39, 39a):

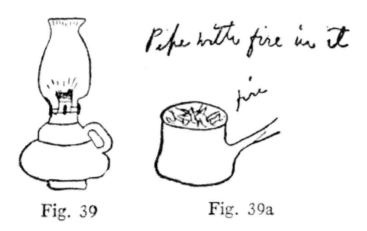

Fig. 39   Fig. 39a

And in series thirty-four another, with comment: "flame and sparks" (figs. 40, 40a):

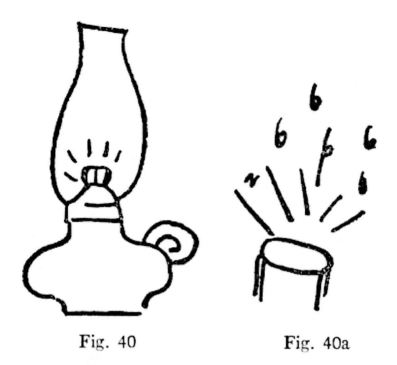

Fig. 40   Fig. 40a

I drew another pipe in series twenty-two, with the usual curls of smoke; and Craig wrote: "Smoke stack." I drew another in series thirty-three with the result that, five drawings in advance of the correct one, Craig drew a pipe with smoke. Of course, this may have been a coincidence; but wait till you see how often such coincidences happen! (figs. 41, 41a):

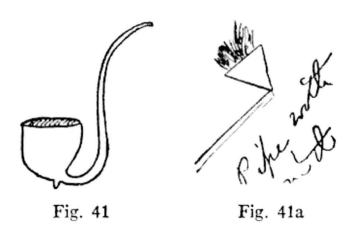

Fig. 41   Fig. 41a

In series twenty-one I drew a chimney, and Craig drew a chimney, and added smoke. In thirty-four I drew an old-fashioned trench-mortar; and here again she supplied the smoke (figs. 42, 42a):

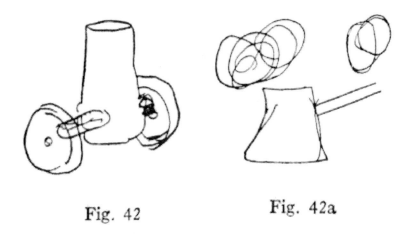

Fig. 42   Fig. 42a

Cannons are especially horrible things to her, as you may note again and again in her published war-sonnets:

The sharpened steel whips round, the black guns blaze, waste are the harvests, mute the songs of birds.

Fig. 43a

So when, in series eleven, I drew the muzzle half of an old-style cannon, Craig's imagination got to work one drawing ahead of time. She wrote: "Fire and smoke—smoke—flame," and then drew as follows (fig. 43a):

The next drawing was the cannon, and I give it, along with the drawing Craig made to go with it. The

67

comment she wrote was: "Half circle —double lines—light inside—light is fire busy whirling or flaming" (figs. 44, 44a):

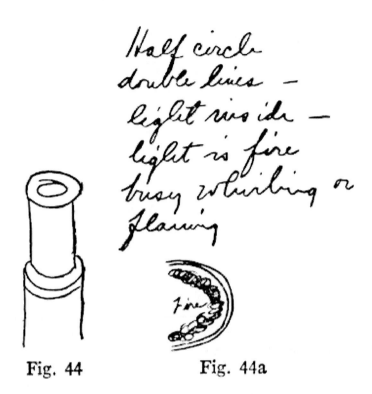

Half circle
double lines —
light inside —
light is fire
busy whirling or
flaming

Fig. 44   Fig. 44a

So much for fires, and things associated with fire. Now consider another detail about life in the Yazoo delta, brought out in the course of our psychoanalysis. In the days of Craig's childhood, poisonous snakes were an ever-present menace, and fear of them had to be taught to children, and could hardly be taught too early. There is a family story of a little tot crawling under the house and coming back to report, "I see nuffin wiv a tail to it!" In the swamps back of Craig's summer home on the Mississippi Sound I have counted a dozen copperheads and moccasins in the course of a half hour's walk. Also, her father has some childhood complex buried in his mind, which causes him to have a spell of nausea at the sight of a snake. All this, of course, strongly affected the child's early days, and now it is in her mental depths. So when I drew a hissing snake, just see the uproar I caused! She made no drawing, but wrote a little essay. I give my drawing, and her essay following (fig. 45):

68

Fig. 45

"See something like kitten with tail and saucer of milk. Now it leaps into action and runs away to outdoors. Turns to fleeing animal outdoors. Great activity among outdoor creatures. Know it's some outdoor thing, not indoor object—see trees, and a frightened bird on the wing (turned sidewise). It's outdoor thing, but none of above seems to be *it.*"

In other words, little Mary Craig Kimbrough is back on the plantation, seeing terror among birds and poultry, and not knowing what causes it! Study the drawing, and you see that I got the action of the snake, but didn't get the coils very well, so they might be a "saucer of milk" —and a sure-enough kitten's tail sticking out from it. Another childhood horror here! Craig was a fat little thing, and she slipped and plumped down on her favorite pet kitten, and exploded it.

XIII

THE person whom we are subjecting to this process of psychoanalysis has a strong color sense, and wanted to be a painter. So we note that she "gets" colors and names them correctly. Here is my drawing of what I meant to be a bouquet of pink roses (figs. 46, 46a):

Fig. 46

Fig. 46a

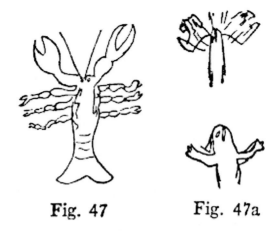

Fig. 47   Fig. 47a

Or take this case of a lobster. Craig's comment was: "Gorgeous colors, red and greenish tinges." Apparently I had failed to decide whether I was drawing a live lobster or a boiled one! My wife wrote further: "Now it turns into a lizard, cameleon (chameleon), reds and greens." When she sees this about to be made public, she is embarrassed by her bad spelling; but she says: "Please do not overlook the fact that a chameleon is a reptile—and so is a lobster." I dutifully quote her, even though her zoology is even worse than her spelling! (figs. 47, 47a):

While we are on the "reptiles," I include this menacing crab, which may have got hold of little Mary Craig's toe on the beach of the Mississippi Sound (fig. 48):

Fig. 48

70

For the crab, Craig made two drawings, on opposite sides of the paper (figs. 48a, 48b):

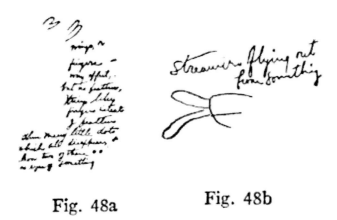

Fig. 48a   Fig. 48b

The comments on the above read: "Wings, or fingers—wing effect, but no feathers, things like fingers instead of feathers. Then many little dots which all disappear, and leave two of them, O O, as eyes of something." And then, "Streamers flying from something."

Another color instance: I drew the head of a horse, and Craig drew a lot of apparently promiscuous lines, and at various places wrote "yellow," "white," "blue," "(dark)," and then a general description, "Oriental." Afterwards she said to me: "That looks like a complete failure; yet it was so vivid, I can't be mistaken. Where did you get that horse?" Said I: "I copied it from a Sunday supplement." We got the paper from the trash-basket, and the page opposite the horse contained what Craig described.

We shall note several other cases of this sort of intrusion of things I did not draw, but which I had before me while drawing.

Also anything with metal or shine seems to stand a good chance of being "got." For example, these nose-glasses (figs. 49, 49a):

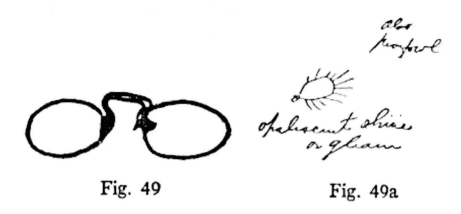

Fig. 49

Fig. 49a

The comment reads: "Opalescent shine or gleam. Also peafowl."

Or again, a belt-buckle; my wife writes the word "shines" (figs. 50, 50a):

Fig. 50

Fig. 50a

Or this very busy alarm clock—she writes the same word "shines" (figs. 51, 51a):

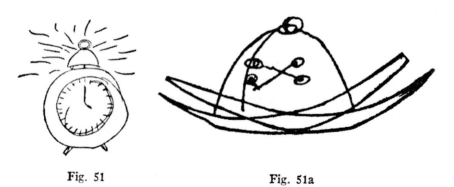

Fig. 51

Fig. 51a

She has got at least part of a watch whenever one has been presented. You remember the one Bob drew (fig. 17). There was another in series thirty-three; Craig made a crude drawing and added: "Shines, glass or metal" (figs. 52, 52a):

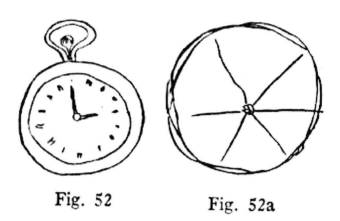

Fig. 52   Fig. 52a

Also, on the automobile ride to Pasadena, series three, there was a watch-face among the drawings, and Craig drew the angle of the hands, and added the words, "a complication of small configurations." Having arrived in Pasadena, she took the twelve drawings and tried them over again. This time, of course, she had a one in twelve chance of guessing the watch. She wrote: "A white translucent glimmering, or shimmering which I knew was not light but rather glass. It was like heat waves radiating in little round pools from a center. . . . Then in the center I saw a vivid black mark. . . . So it was bound to be the watch, and it was."

And here is a fountain. You see that it appears to be in a tub, and is so drawn by Craig. But you note that the "shine" has been got. "These shine!" (figs. 53, 53a):

Fig. 53   Fig. 53a

Another instance, even more vivid. I made a poor attempt to draw a bass tuba, as one sees them on the stage—a lot of jazz musicians dressed up in white duck, and a row of big brass and nickel horns, polished to blind your eyes. See what Craig drew, and also what she wrote (figs. 54, 54a):

Fig. 54   Fig. 54a

Fig. 54, Fig 54a

The comments, continued on the other side of the sheet, are: "Dull gold ring shimmers and stands out with shadow behind it and in center of it. Gleams and moves. Metal. There is a glow of gold light,

74

and the ring or circle is out in the air, suspended, and moves in blur of gold."

You see, she gets the feeling, the emotional content. I draw a child's express-wagon, and she writes: "Children again playing but can't get exactly how they look. Just feel there are children." Or take this one, which she describes as "Egyptian." I don't know if my pillar is real

Egyptian, but it seems so to me, and evidently to my wife, for you note all the artistry it inspired (figs. 55, 55a):

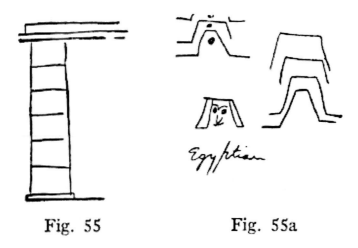

Fig. 55   Fig. 55a

Sometimes Craig will embody the feeling in some new form of her own invention; as for example, when I draw an old-fashioned cannon on wheels, and she writes: "Black Napoleon hat and red military coat." I draw a running fox —well drawn, because I copy it from a picture; she rises to the occasion with two crossed guns, and a hunting horn with a lot of musical notes coming out of it (figs. 56, 56a):

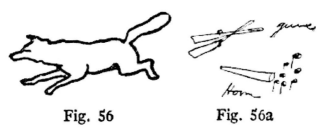

Fig. 56   Fig. 56a

I draw an auto, and she replies with the hub and spokes of a wheel. Not satisfied with this, she sets it aside, and tries again a little later—without looking at the original drawing—and this time she produces a horn, with indication of a noise. I give both her drawings, which are on two sides of the same slip of paper (figs. 57a, 57b):

Fig. 57a

Fig. 57b

XIV

AN extraordinary incident occurred in connection with the fourth series of drawings. While my secretary, E. M. Hart, was making the drawings, there came into the office his brother-in-law, R. H. Craig, Jr., a teller of the Security First National Bank of Long Beach, a person entirely unknown to my wife. He heard what was going on, and said, "I'll give her some that'll stump her." He took a pen and drew two pictures, which were duly wrapped in sheets of green paper and sealed in envelopes, and put with the rest of the series. I was not at the office, and nothing was said to me about Mr. Craig having taken part in the matter.

My wife did this series under my eyes; and when she came to the first of Mr. Craig's two drawings, she wrote, "Some sort of grinning monster," and added an elaborate description. Then she opened the envelope, and found a roller skate with a foot and leg attached. This, naturally, was called a failure; but seven drawings later in the same series came Mr. Craig's other drawing, which was as follows (fig. 58):

Fig. 58

Now read the amazing description, which my wife had written, seven drawings back, when the first of Mr. Craig's drawings had come under her hand:

"Some sort of grinning monster—see only the face and a vague idea of deformed neck and shoulders. It is a man, but it looks like a cat's face, cat eyes and whiskers. Don't know just how I know it is a man—it is a deformity. Not a cat. See color of skin which is deep, flat pink, as of a colored picture. The face of the creature is broad and weird. The flesh of neck, or somewhere, gives effect of rolls or creases."

I asked my secretary what this drawing was meant to be, and he said "a Happy Hooligan."

My cultural backwardness is such that I wasn't sure just what a "Happy Hooligan" might be, but my secretary told me it is a comic supplement figure, and I then looked it up in the paper, and found that the face of the figure as printed is a very pale pink, and the little cap on top is a bright red. I called Mr. Craig on the phone and asked him this question: "If you were to think of a color in connection with a 'Happy Hooligan,' what color would it be?" He answered, "Red."

Now I ask you, what chance do you think there is of a person's writing a description such as the above by guess work? To be sure, my wife had eight guesses; but do you think that eight million guesses would suffice? And if we call it telepathy, do we say that my wife's mind has the power to dip into the mind of a young man whom she has never seen, nor even heard of? Or shall we say that his mind affected his brother-in-law's, the brother-in-law's affected mine, and mine affected my wife's? Or, if we decide to call it clairvoyance, or psychometry, then are we going to say there is some kind of vibration or emanation from Mr. Craig's drawing, so powerful that when one of his drawings is handed to my wife, she gets what is in another drawing which has been done at the same time?

Whatever may be the explanation, here is the fact: Again and again we find Craig getting, not the drawing she is holding under her hand, but the next one, which she has not yet touched. When she picks up the first drawing, she will say, or write: "There is a little man in this series"; or: "There is a snow scene with sled"; or: "An elephant, also a rooster." I am going to show you these particular cases; but first a word as to how I have counted such "anticipations."

Manifestly, if I grant the right to more than one guess, I am increasing the chances of guesswork, and correspondingly reducing the significance of the totals. What I have done is this: where such cases have occurred, I have called them total failures, except in a few cases, where the description was so detailed and exact as to be overwhelming—as in the case of this "Happy Hooligan." Even so, I have not called it a complete success, only a partial success. In order to be classified as a complete success, my wife's drawing must have been made for the particular drawing of mine which she had in her hand at that time; and throughout this account, the reader is to understand that every drawing presented was made in connection with the particular drawing printed alongside it—except in cases where I expressly state otherwise.

Now for a few of the "anticipations." In the course of series six, drawn by me on Feb. 8, 1929, drawing number two was a daisy, and Craig got the elements of it, as you see (figs. 59. 59a):

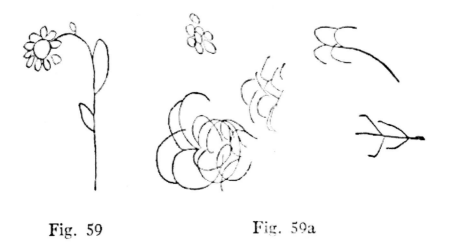

Fig. 59   Fig. 59a

Her mind then went ahead, and she wrote, "May be snow scene on hill and sled." The next drawing was an axe, which I give later (fig. 145); she got the elements of this very well, and then added, on the back: "I get a feeling again of a snow scene to come in this series—a sled in the snow." That was number three; and when number five came Craig made this annotation: "Opened it by mistake, without concentrating.

It's my expected sled and snow scene." Here is the drawing (fig. 60):

Fig. 60

Series number eight, on Feb. 10, brought even stranger results. This is the series in which the laced-up football was turned into a calf wearing a belly-band (figs. 15, 15a). But even while I was engaged in making the drawings, sitting in my study apart, and with the door closed, Craig's busy magic, whatever it is, was bringing her messages. She called out: "I see a rooster!" I had actually drawn a rooster; but of course I made no reply to her words. She at once drew a rooster and several other things, and after I had brought my drawings into the room, but before she had started co work with them, she wrote as follows:

"While Upton was making these drawings I sat before the fire thinking how to dry felt slippers which I had washed. I had my mind on them. Hung them on grating to see if they would hang there without burning. Suddenly saw rooster crowing. Then thought, 'Can U be drawing rooster?' Decided to make note of this.

Did so. Then saw"—and she draws a circle with eight radiating lines, like spokes of a wheel.

In due course came drawing number eight, and before looking at it, Craig wrote: "Rooster." Then she added, "But no—it looks like a picture of coffee-pot—see spout and handle." This is hard on me as an artist, but I give the drawing and let you judge for yourself (fig. 61):

Fig. 61

What about the circle and the radiating spokes? That was, apparently, a fore-glimpse of drawing number five. I give you that, together with what Craig drew for that particular test when it came. Her effort suggests the kind of humor with which the newspaper artists used to delight my childhood; a series of drawings in which one thing turns into some other and quite unexpected thing by gradual changes. You will see here how the hub of a wagon-wheel may turn into the muzzle of a deer! (figs. 62, 62a):

80

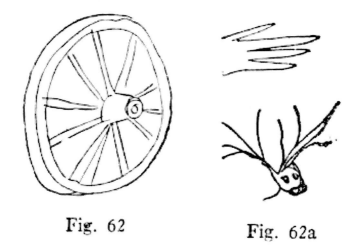

Fig. 62   Fig. 62a

XV

WHAT are the principles upon which I have classified the drawings, as between successes, partial successes, and failures? I will use this series, number eight, to illustrate. There are eight drawings, and I have set them down as one success, six partial successes, one failure. The success is the rooster (fig. 61), called "a rooster," even though it "looks like a coffee pot." The partial successes are, first, an electric light bulb, very crudely imitated as to shape in three drawings. Perhaps this was hardly good enough to be counted; it was a border-line case, and probably the poorest that I admitted to the classification of "partial successes" (fig. 63a).

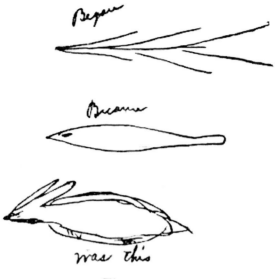

Fig. 63a

Second, the ascending sky-rocket, already printed as fig. 38, giving rise to six different drawings of whirligigs and light. Third, the following drawing, for which Craig wrote: "See spider, or some sort of legged pest. If this is not a spider, there is a spider in the lot somewhere!
This I know!"
(fig. 64):

The fourth partial success was a drawn bow, with arrow fitted, ready to be launched. Craig wrote as follows: "Picked this up and saw inside as it dropped on floor—so did not try it. Suddenly recall I have

Fig. 64

already 'seen' it earlier." Before starting the tests, along with her written mention of "a rooster," she had drawn a bow and crude arrow, and the resemblance is so exact that it seems to me entitled to be called a partial success (figs. 65, 65a):

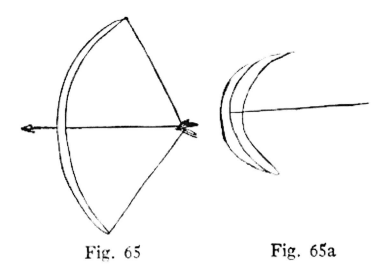

Fig. 65   Fig. 65a

Fifth, the wagon hub (fig. 60), which became the deer's muzzle. And finally the laced-up football (fig. 15) which became a belly-band on a calf (fig. 15a).

As for the failure in this series, it is a cake of soap, which was called "whirls." There are a couple of other drawings in the series, marked: "Too tired to see it," and "Tired now and excited and keep seeing old things"—meaning, of course, the preceding drawings.

I tried to avoid drawing the same object more than once, but now and then I slipped up. In series eleven I drew another rooster, and there followed, not one "anticipation," but several. Drawing number one was a tooth; Craig wrote: "First see rooster. Then elephant." Drawing number two was an elephant; and Craig wrote: "Elephant came again. I try to suppress it, and see lines, and a spike sticking some way into something." She drew it, and it seems clear that the "spike" is the elephant's tusk, and the head of the "spike" is the elephant's eye (figs. 66, 66a):

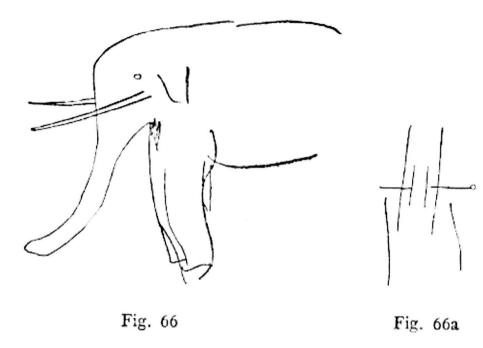

Fig. 66   Fig. 66a

Next, number three, was the rooster. But Craig had set "rooster"
down in her mind as a blunder, so now she wrote: "I don't know
what, see a bunch, or tuft clearly. Also a crooked arm on a body.
But don't feel that I'm right." Here are the drawings, and you can
see that she was somewhat right (figs. 67, 67a):

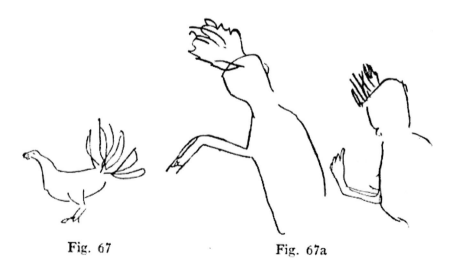

Fig. 67   Fig. 67a

This series eleven, containing fourteen drawings, is marked: "Did this lot rapidly, without holding (mind) blank. The chicken and elephant came *at once*, on a very earnest request to my mind to 'come across.'" I have classified in this series two successes, five partial, and five failures: throwing out numbers twelve and fourteen, because Craig wrote: "Nothing except all the preceding ones come—too many at once—all past ones crowding in memory"; and again, "Nothing but everything in the preceding. Too many of them in my mind."

The anticipations run all through this series in a quite fascinating way. Thus, for number four Craig wrote: "Flower. This is a very vivid one. Green spine—leaves like century plant." She drew figure 68a:

Fig. 68a

And then again, for drawing number seven, she did more flowers, with this comment: "This is a *real* flower, I've seen it before. It's vivid and returns. Century plant? Now it turns into candle stick. See a candle" (fig. 69a).

All this was wrong—so far. Number four was a table, and number seven was the rear half of a cow. But now we come to number eleven, the plant known as a "cat-tail," which seems to resemble rather surprisingly the lower of the two drawings in figure 69a. My drawing is given as figure 70, and the one Craig made for it is given as 70a.

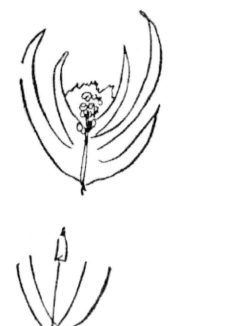

Candle stick.
a candle

Fig. 69a

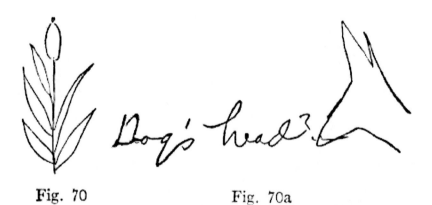

Fig. 70   Fig. 70a

Comment on the above read: "Very pointed. Am not able to see what. Dog's head?"

86

Drawing five was a large fish-hook; and this inspired the experimenter to a discourse, as follows: "Dog wagging—see tail in air busy wagging—jolly doggie—tail curled in air." And then: "Now I see a cow. I fear the elephant and chicken got me too sure of animals. But I see these."

Now, a big fish-hook looks not unlike a "tail curled in air." But when we come to number seven, we discover what Craig was apparently anticipating. It is the drawing of what I have referred to as "the rear half of a cow." It is badly done, with a cow's hoof, but I forgot what a cow's tail is like, and this tail that I drew would fit much better on a "jolly doggy," you must admit (fig. 71):

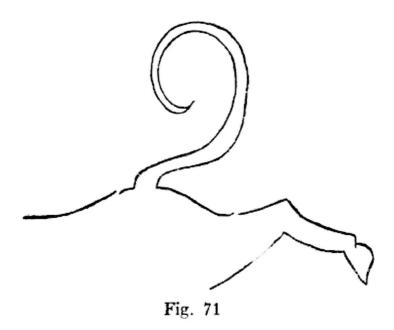

Fig. 71

Drawing number six was a sun, as children draw it, a circle with rays going out all round. Craig wrote: "Setting sun and bird in sky. Big bird on wing—seagull or wild goose." This I called a partial success. Number nine was the muzzle end of an old-style cannon, already reported in figs. 46, 46a.

I conclude the study of this particular series with drawing thirteen, to which was added the comment: "Think of a saucer, then of a cup. It's something in the kitchen. Too tired to see" (figs. 72, 72a):

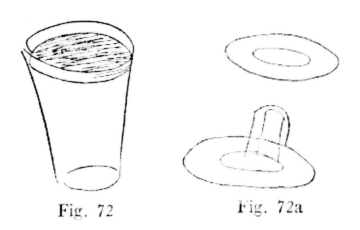

Fig. 72   Fig. 72a

In series fourteen, drawing three, Craig wrote: "Man running, can't draw it." She drew as follows (fig. 73a):	Next came my drawing four, as follows (fig. 73):

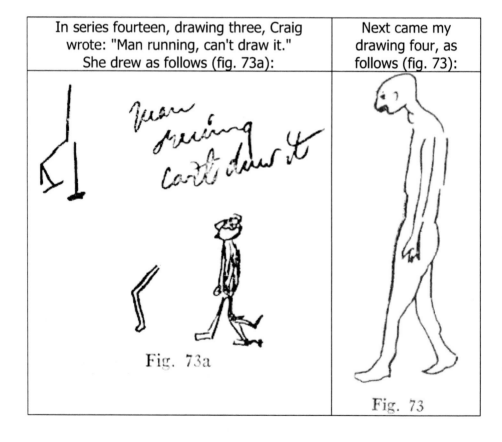

Fig. 73a

Fig. 73

In series thirty-five I first drew a fire hydrant, and Craig wrote, "Peafowl," and added the following drawing, which certainly constitutes a partial success (figs. 74, 74a):

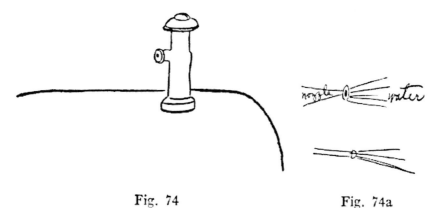

Fig. 74   Fig. 74a

My next drawing was the peafowl, as you see. For this Craig wrote: "Peafowl again," and apparently tried to draw the peafowl's neck, and a lot of those spots which I had forgotten are an appurtenance of peafowls (figs. 75, 75a):

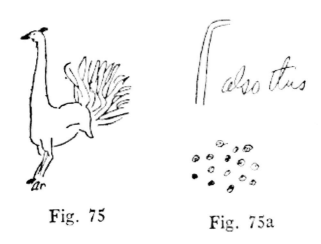

Fig. 75   Fig. 75a

In series twenty-nine I drew an elevated railway. If you turn it upside down, as I have done here, it looks like water and smoke-stacks. Anyhow, Craig drew a steamboat (figs. 76, 76a):

89

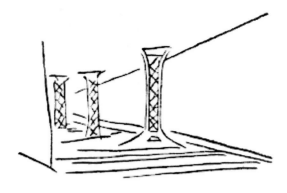

Fig. 76

Fig. 76a

And then came my next drawing—a steamboat! Craig wrote: "Smoke again," and drew the smoke and the stack (figs. 77, 77):

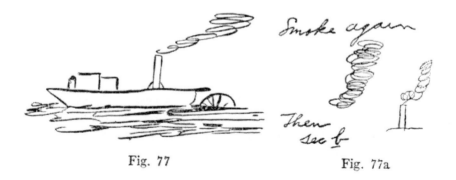

Fig. 77

Fig. 77a

She added two more drawings, which appear to be the wheel of the boat in the water, and the smoke (figs. 77b, 77c):

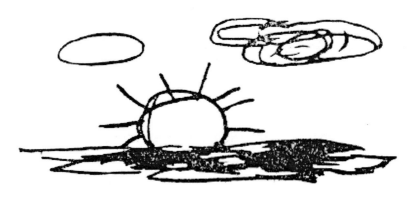

Fig. 77b

Fig. 77c

In series thirty I drew a fish-hook with line, and you see it turned into a flower (figs. 78, 78a);

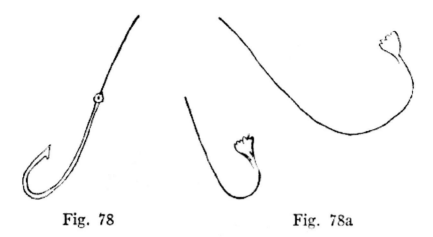

Fig. 78   Fig. 78a

Then came an obelisk, and Craig got it, but with novel effects, thus (figs. 79, 79a):

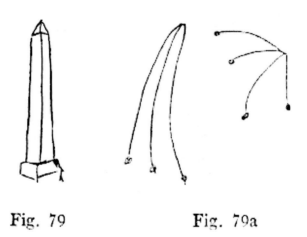

Fig. 79   Fig. 79a

Now why should an obelisk go on a jag, and have little circles at its base? The answer appears to be: it inherited the curves from the previous fish-hook, and the little circles from the next drawing. You will see that, having used up her supply of little circles, Craig did not get the next drawing so well (figs. 80, 80a):

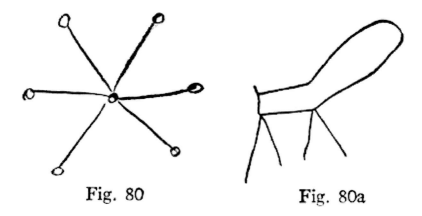

Fig. 80   Fig. 80a

In series twenty-two I first drew a bed, and Craig made two attempts to draw a potted plant. My second drawing was a maltese cross, and Craig turned it into a basket (figs. 81, 81a):

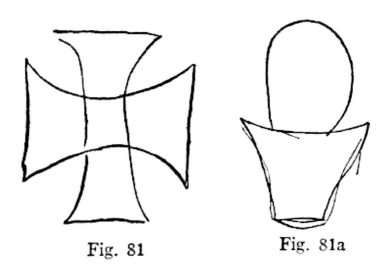

Fig. 81   Fig. 81a

But she could not give up her plant. She added: "There is a flower basket in this lot, or potted plant." The next drawing was a fleur-de-lys, which looks not unlike a potted plant or hanging basket (fig. 82):

Fig. 82

In drawing four she got the elements of a door-knob pretty well, and added: "See head of bird, too—eagle beak." Drawing seven was a crane, with beak open.

XVI

I COULD go through all thirty-five of the series, listing such "anticipations" as this: but I have given enough to show how the thing goes. Such occurrences make it hard for Craig because, when she has once drawn a certain object, she naturally resists the impulse to draw it again, thinking it is nothing but a memory. Thus, in series thirteen, my first drawing was a savage woman carrying a bundle on her head, and Craig drew the profile of a head with a long nose. My next drawing was the profile of a head, with a very conspicuous nose, and Craig wrote: "Face again, but (I) inhibit this. Then come two hands, and below"—and she draws what might be a cross section of a skull, side view.

Yet sometimes she overcomes this handicap triumphantly. Series twelve is marked: "Hastily done," and she adds the general comment: "Several times saw bristles on things of different shapes, some flowers, some bristled brushes. Saw flower, also more than once"—and then she appends a drawing of a four-leaf clover. As it

94

happened, this series contained a three-leaf clover, and it contained another flower, and also a cactus-plant—more of one kind of thing than it was fair to put into one set of drawings. Nevertheless, Craig scored one of her successes with the cactus, setting it down as "fuzzy flower" (figs. 83, 83a):

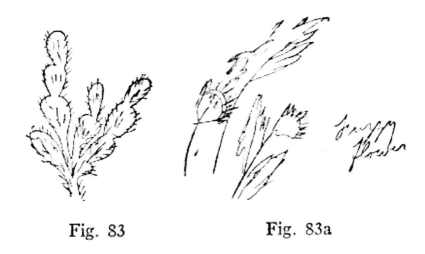

Fig. 83   Fig. 83a

Nor was she afraid to repeat herself when she came to another "fuzzy flower" in this series (figs. 84, 84a):

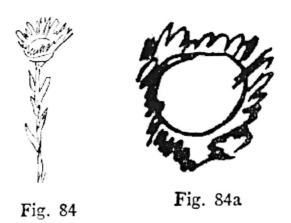

Fig. 84

Fig. 84a

Frequently she will make a good drawing of an object, but name it badly. In that same series twelve I drew a hoe, and she got the shape of it, but wrote: "May be scissors, may be spectacles with long stem ears" (figs. 85, 85a):

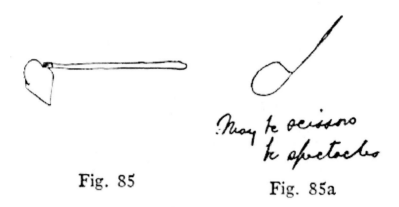

Fig. 85

Fig. 85a

Also in the same series these reindeer horns, which she calls "holly leaves." It is psychologically interesting to note that reindeer and holly trees were both associated with Christmas in Craig's childhood (figs. 86, 86a):

Fig. 86

Fig. 86a

And in series eighteen, this fat baby bird of mine is hardly recognizable when called "flounder" (figs. 87, 87a):

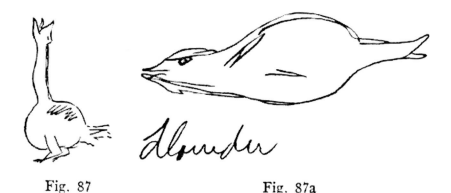

Fig. 87   Fig. 87a

This very dim stalk of celery, drawn by me, I must admit looks more like a fish-fork (figs. 88, 88a):

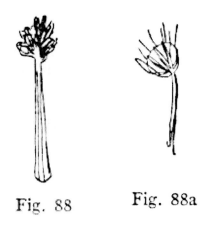

Fig. 88   Fig. 88a

Craig's verbal description of the above reads: "Stone set in platinum; may be diamond, as points seem to be white light—at least it shines, not red shine of fire but white shine." How does a stalk of celery, which looks like a fish-fork, come to have a diamond set in it? You may understand the reason when you hear that three drawings later in the same series is a diamond set in a stick. Just why it occurred to me to set a diamond thus I cannot now recall, but the drawing is plain, and it led to a bit of fun. I had been to lunch with Charlie Chaplin that day, and had come home and told my wife about it; so here my sparkling diamond undergoes a transfiguration! "Chaplin," writes my wife, and adds: "I don't see why he has on a halo" (figs. 89, 89):

97

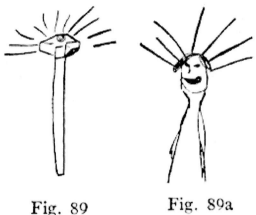

Fig. 89   Fig. 89a

From the point of view of bad guessing, the most conspicuous series is number twenty. In this I have recorded four successes, seven partial, and one failure; yet there is hardly an object that is correctly named. Here are the three which I call successes; there may be dispute about any one of them, but it seems to me the essential elements have been got. You may be surprised at a necktie which "began to smoke" —but not when you see that the next drawing is a burning match! (Figs. 90, 90a; 91, 91a; 92, 92a):

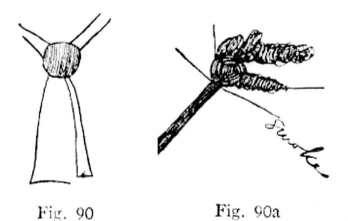

Fig. 90   Fig. 90a

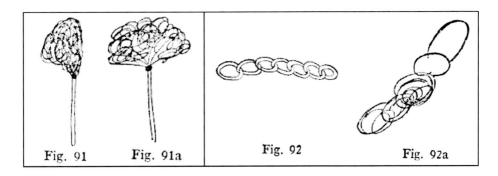

| Fig. 91 | Fig. 91a | Fig. 92 | Fig. 92a |

As for the partial successes, I give six of them by way of samples. For the first, Craig's comment was: "The body is vague, but see there is a body." You will agree that my mountain landscape looks oddly like a body (figs. 93, 93a):

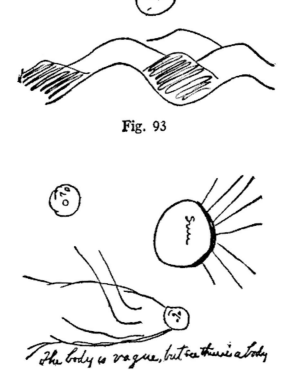

Fig. 93

Fig. 93a

And the pedals of this harp make a charming pair of lady's feet (figs, 94, 94a):

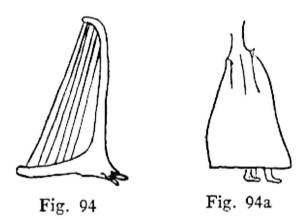

Fig. 94   Fig. 94a

This balloon is described in my wife's comment as: "Shines in sunlight, must be metal, a scythe hanging among vines or strings."

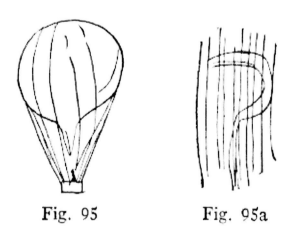

Fig. 95   Fig. 95a

This, which is called "front foot and leg of dog, though I don't see the dog," is really drawn more like the spigot of my drawing (figs. 96, 96a):

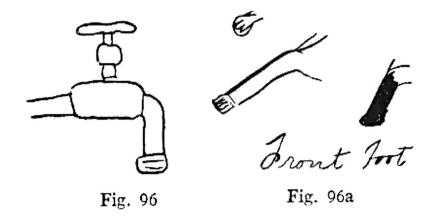

Fig. 96   Fig. 96a

A butterfly's wings are "got" remarkably well (figs. 97, 97a). And the trade-marks on my little box are called "tiny stars. or sparks" (figs. 98, 98a):

Fig. 97   Fig. 97a

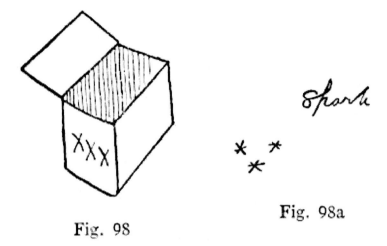

Fig. 98

Fig. 98a

XVII

I HAVE referred to the fact that my wife's drawings sometimes contain things which are not in mine, but which were in my mind while I was making them, or while she was "concentrating." One of the most curious of such cases came in series twenty-eight, which was after we had given up, as too great a nuisance, all precautions in the way of sealing the drawings in envelopes. I made eight drawings, and laid them face down on my wife's table, and then went out and took a walk while she did them. So, of course, it was easy for her to do what she pleased—and maybe she "peeked," the skeptic will say. But as it happens, she didn't get a single one right! Instead of reproducing my drawings, what she did was to reproduce my thoughts while I was walking up and down on the ocean front. It seems to me that in so doing, she provided a perfect answer to those who may attribute these results to any form of deception, whether conscious or unconscious.

There was a moon behind a bank of dark clouds, and it produced an unusual effect—a well-defined white cross in the sky. I watched it for nearly half an hour, and my continued thought was: "If this were an age of superstition, that would be a portent, and we should hear about it in history." It was so strange that I finally went home and called my wife out onto the street. I did not tell her why.

I wanted to see her surprise, so I purposely gave no hint. I said: "Come out! Please come!" Finally she came, and her comment was: "I just drew that!" We went back into the house, and she handed me a drawing. I give it alongside my drawing of an Indian club, which Craig had held while doing hers. You may see exactly how much of her impulse came from that source (figs. 99, 99a):

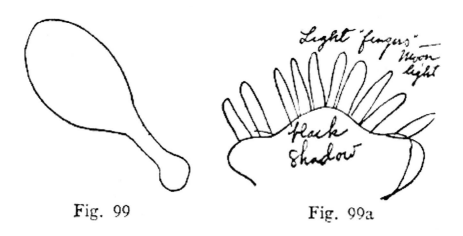

Fig. 99   Fig. 99a

The "comment" reads: "Light 'fingers'—moonlight." Also: "black shadow."

Let me add also that in the eight drawings I handed to Craig there was neither moon, cloud, cross, nor light. Two of these eight my wife failed to mark, and so I cannot identify them as belonging to this series; but we examined all eight at the time, and made sure of this point. Those which I now have are a flag, a bearded man, a chiffonier, a cannon, a dirt-scraper, and the Indian club, given above.

You will ask, perhaps, did Craig look out of the window. As it happened, this sky effect was invisible from any window, and I have her word that she had not moved from her couch. I should add that she is nervous, and keeps the curtains tightly drawn at night, and never goes out at night unless it is to be driven somewhere. It was early in March, with a cold wind off the sea, and I had to labor to persuade her to put a wrap over her dressing gown and step out into the middle of the street to look up at the sky.

XVIII

THE casual reader may be bored by too many of these drawings, but they are easy to skip, or to take in at a glance, and there may be students who will want to examine them carefully. So I will add a selection of the significant drawings, with only brief remarks. I begin with what I have called partial successes, and then add a few more of those I have called "complete."

Let us return to the early drawings, made by my secretary. On the automobile ride to Pasadena, there was an ash-can (fig. 100):

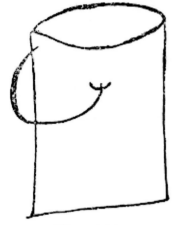

For the above my wife wrote: "I see a chain dangling from something— resembling little chimney pot on top of house."

And here is design for which the comment was: "These somehow belong together but won't get together" (figs. 101, 101a):

Fig. 100

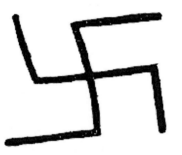

Fig. 101

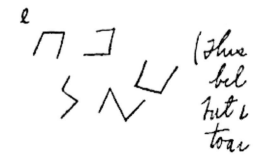

Fig. 101a

104

Here is a fan, with comment: "Inside seems irregular, as if cloth draped or crumpled" (figs. 102, 102a):

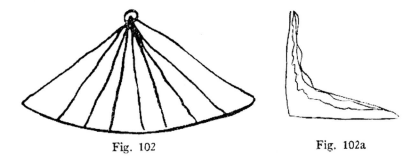

Fig. 102   Fig. 102a

Here is a one-half success (figs. 103, 103a):

Fig. 103   Fig. 103a   Here is a broom, drawn by my secretary (fig. 104), and several efforts to reproduce it

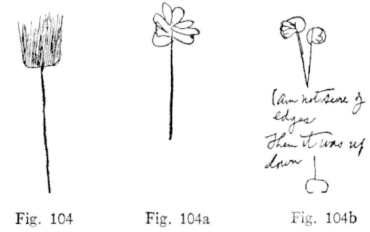

Fig. 104   Fig. 104a   Fig. 104b

(figs. 104a, 104b):

The comments accompanying these drawings read: "All I'm sure of is a straight line with something curved at end of it; once it came" (here is drawing of the flower). "Then it doubled, or reappeared, I don't know which. (Am not sure of curly edges.) Then it was upside down."

The next drawing was a heart, and my wife got the upper half with what are apparently blood-drops added (figs. 105, 105a):

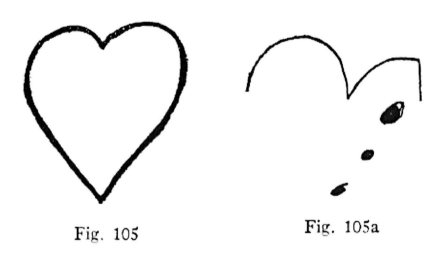

Fig. 105   Fig. 105a

The above is interesting, as suggesting that whatever agency furnished the information knew more than it was telling. For if Craig's drawing, a pair of curves, constituted a crude letter N, or had no significance, why add the blood-drops, which were not in the original? On the other hand, if her subconscious mind knew it was a heart, why not give her the whole heart, and let her draw it?

So much for the drawings of my secretary; and now for my own early drawings. When I was a school boy, we used to represent human figures in this way; and, as you see, Craig got the essentials (figs. 106, 106a):

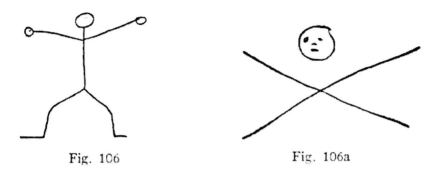

Fig. 106

Fig. 106a

Several weeks later, I drew a pair of such figures in action and the comment was: "It's a whirligig of some sort" (figs. 107, 107a).

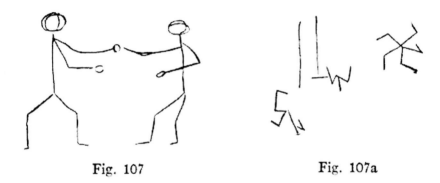

Fig. 107

Fig. 107a

After the following drawing, Craig asked me not to do any more hands, for the reason that she "got" this, but thought it was my own hand doing the drawing. She guessed something else, and wrote: "Turned into pig's head, then rabbit's" (figs. 108, 108a):

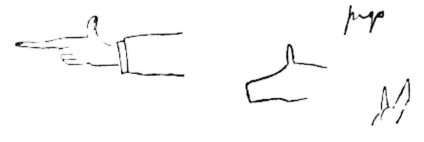

Fig. 108

Fig. 108a

Next, this bat, with very striking comment.

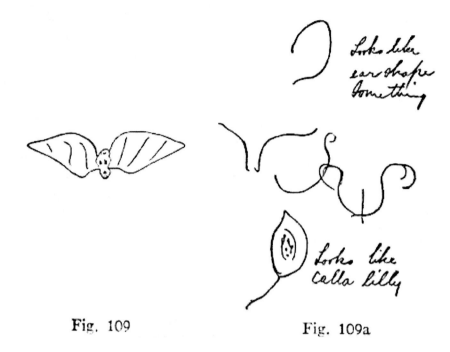

Fig. 109   Fig. 109a

"Looks like ear-shaped something," and again: "Looks like calla lily" (figs. 109, 109a):

A butterfly net (fig. 110, 110a).

Fig. 110   Fig. 110a

A key (figs. 111, 111a):

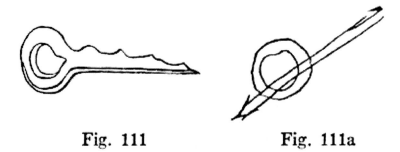

Fig. 111   Fig. 111a

This highly humorous sunrise (figs. 112, 112a):

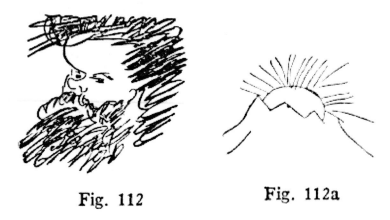

Fig. 112   Fig. 112a

A carnation which came after the preceding drawing, and apparently had been anticipated in the "sunrise" (figs. 113, 113a).

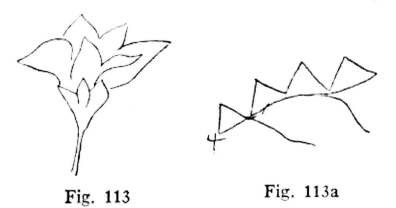

Fig. 113   Fig. 113a

Note that this camp-stool, as I drew it, really does appear to be standing on water (figs. 114, 114a):

Fig. 114   Fig. 114a

For this little waiter, who follows, no drawing was made by my wife. Her written comment was: "I see at once the profile of human face. Am interrupted by radio tune. Something makes me think of a cow. Now see two things sticking out like horns" (figs. 115).

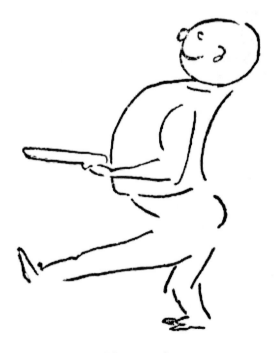

Fig. 115

The following had no comment (figs. 116, 116a):

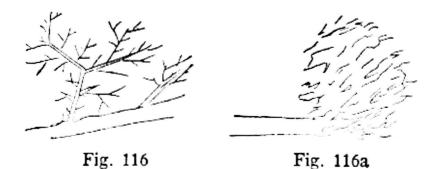

Fig. 116   Fig. 116a

Nor the next one (figs. 117, 117a):

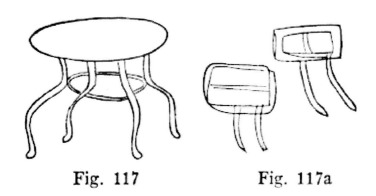

Fig. 117   Fig. 117a

The comment on this caterpillar was: "Fork —then garden tool— lawn rake. Leaf." I might add that we have a lawn-rake made of bristly bamboo, which looks very much like my drawing (figs. 118, 118a):

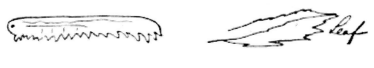

Fig. 118   Fig. 118a

In the following case I drew sixteen stars, and you may count and see that Craig got twelve of them, and made up the difference with a moon! (figs. 119, 119a):

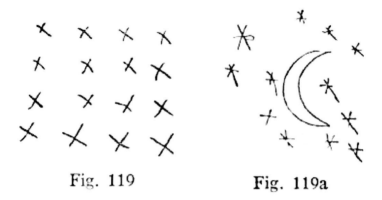

Fig. 119   Fig. 119a

Comment on the following: "Looks like a monkey wrench, but it may be a yardstick" (figs. 120, 120a):

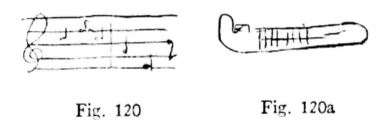

Fig. 120   Fig. 120a

In the next one, the curve of the worm is amusingly reproduced by the bird's neck. The comment added: "But it may be a snake." Craig says this is an example of how one part of the drawing comes to her, and then, in haste, her memory-trains and associations supply what they think should be the rest (figs. 121, 121a).

112

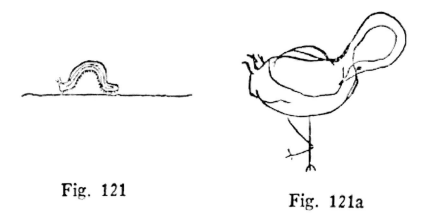

Fig. 121   Fig. 121a

The umbrella brings up Craig's reptile "complex" again. I assure you that in her garden, she turns sticks into snakes when they are far less snake-like than my drawing. Her comment was: "I feel that it is a snake crawling out of something—vivid feeling of snake, but it looks like a cat's tail" (figs. 122, 122a):

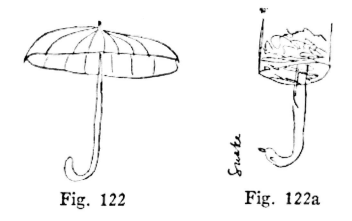

Fig. 122   Fig. 122a

I drew a wall-hook to hang your coat on (figs. 123, 123a):

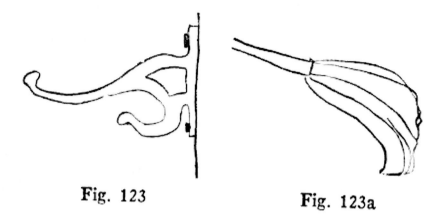

Fig. 123   Fig. 123a

A design, evidently felt as a design, though not well got (figs. 124, 124a):

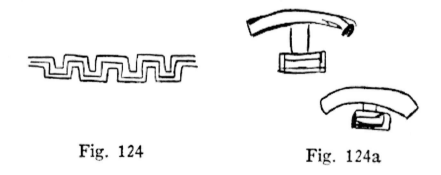

Fig. 124   Fig. 124a

A screw, with comment: "light-house or tower. Too fat at base." If Craig's drawing were made narrower at base, it would reproduce the screw very well. Note that in the right-hand "tower" the screw-like effect of the "set backs" is kept (figs. 125, 125a):

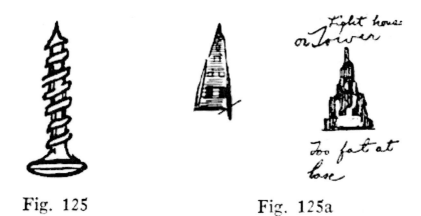

Fig. 125   Fig. 125a

Fig. 125, Fig. 125a

Here is a love story which seems to go wrong, the hearts being turned to opposition (figs. 126, 126a):

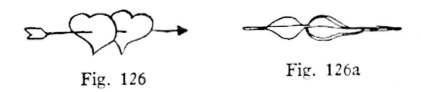

Fig. 126   Fig. 126a

Here is the flag, made simpler—"e pluribus unum!" (figs. 127, 127a):

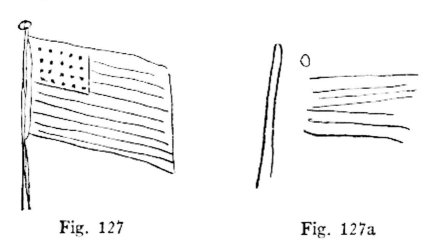

Fig. 127   Fig. 127a

115

Here is a cow, as seen by the cubists. Comment: "Something sending out long lines from it" (figs. 128, 128a):

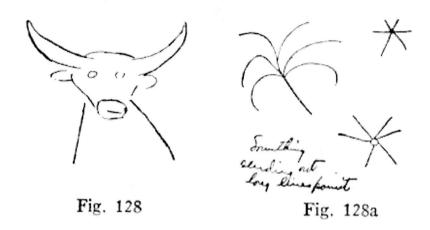

Fig. 128   Fig. 128a

Telegraph wires, apparently seen as waves in the ether (figs. 129, 129a):

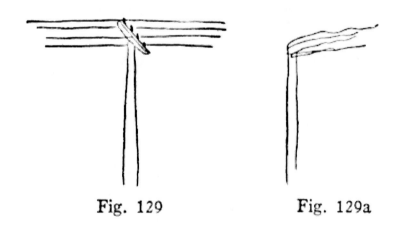

Fig. 129   Fig. 129a

Comment on the following: "Horns. Can't see what they are attached to" (figs. 130, 130a):

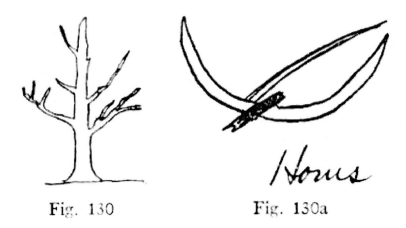

Fig. 130   Fig. 130a

And here is a parrot turned into a leaf, with comment. "See veins and stem with sharp vivid bend in it"—which seems to indicate a sense of the parrot's beak (figs. 131, 131a):

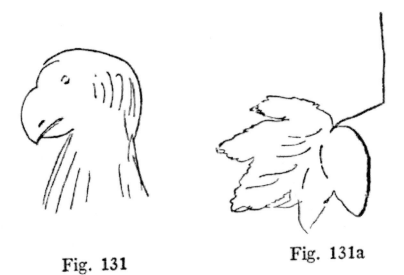

Fig. 131   Fig. 131a

XIX

THE border-line between successes and failures is not easy to determine. Bear in mind that we are not conducting a drawing class, nor making tests of my wife's eyesight: we are trying to ascertain whether there does pass from my mind to hers, or from my drawing to her mind, a recognizable impulse of some sort. So, if she gets the essential feature of the drawing, we are entitled to call it evidence of telepathy. I think the fan with "crumpled cloth" (fig. 102), and the umbrella handle that may be a "snake crawling out of something," but that "looks like a cat's tail" (fig. 122), and the screw that was called a "tower" (fig. 125)—all these are really successes. I will append a number of examples, about which there seems to me no room for dispute, and which I have called successes. The first is a sample of architecture (figs. 132, 132a):

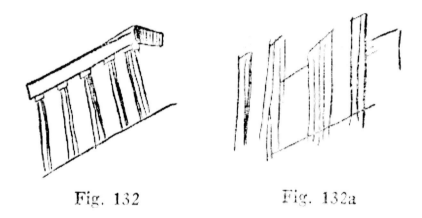

Fig. 132   Fig. 132a

And here is an hour-glass, with sand running through it. Not merely did Craig write "white sand," but she made the tree the same shape as the glass. I have turned the hour-glass upside down so that you can get the effect better. It should be obvious that "upside-downness" has nothing to do with these tests, as Craig is as apt to be holding a drawing one way as another (figs. 133, 133a):

118

Fig. 133   Fig. 133a

And these three circles, with comment: "Feel sure it is," written above the drawing (figs. 134, 134a):

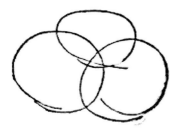

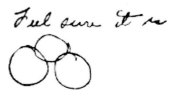

Fig. 134   Fig. 134a

As to the next comment, "Trumpet flower," let me explain that we have them in our garden, whereas we do not have any musical trumpets or horns (figs. 135, 135a):

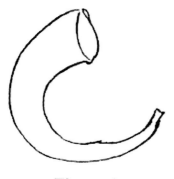

Fig. 135   Fig. 135a

This strange object from my pencil tried to be a conch-shell, but got a bad start, and was left unclassified. Craig made it "life bouy in water," which is good, except for the spelling. She insists upon my pointing out that shells also belong in water (figs. 136, 136a):

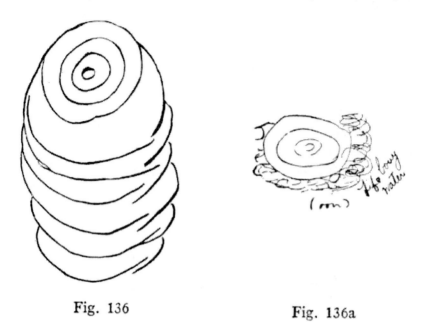

Fig. 136   Fig. 136a

This one, described in good country fashion, "Muley cow with tongue hanging out" (fig. 137):

Fig. 137

This next one was described by the written word: "Goat" (fig. 138):

Fig. 138

And this one is so striking that I give the words in facsimile (figs. 139, 139a):

Fig. 139   Fig. 139a

For the following, my wife described a wrong thing, and then added: "Now a sudden new thing, cone-shaped or goblet-like. This feels like *it*" (figs. 140, 140a):

Fig. 140   Fig. 140a

This was correctly named: "2 legs of something running" (figs. 141, 141a):

Fig. 141

Fig. 141a

This Alpine hat with feather seems to me no less a success because it is called "Chafing dish" (figs. 142, 142a):

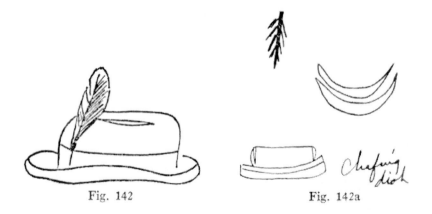

Fig. 142   Fig. 142a

Nor this wind-mill because the sails are left off (figs. 143, 143a):

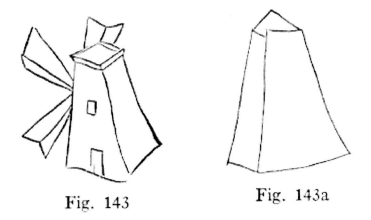

Fig. 143   Fig. 143a

These concentric circles are called "Horn (very curled), or shell" (figs. 144, 144a):

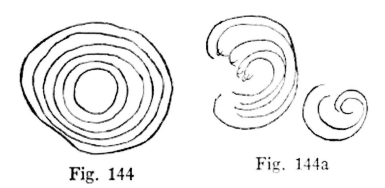

Fig. 144   Fig. 144a

And here is a curious one, which came early in the tests. I call attention to the comment about the handle, which ran off the sheet of paper without any ending, just as she says. "Letter A with something long above it. Key or a sword, there seems to be no end to the handle. Think it's a key" (figs. 145, 145a):

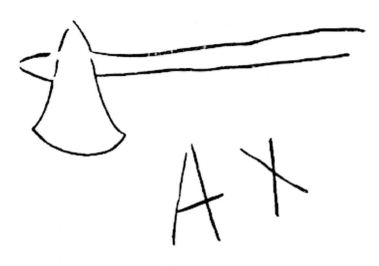

Fig. 145

Letter A with something long above it

a key or sword, there seem to be no

end to handle think its a key

Fig. 145a

And finally, this still more astonishing one, to serve as a climax. Let me explain that I am not so good an artist as this; I copied my drawing from some magazine (figs. 146, 146a):

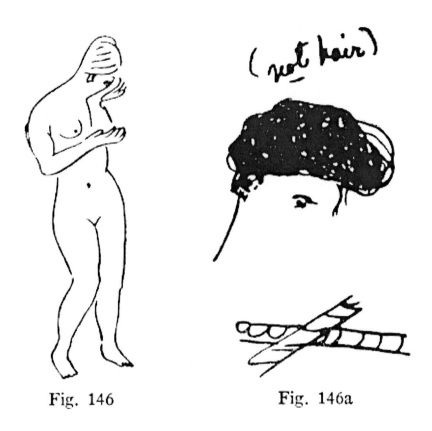

Fig. 146   Fig. 146a

You note that my wife "got," not merely the whole top of the drawing, but some impression of the arms, which are crossed in a peculiar way. I ask her about this case—the drawing having been made less than a month ago—and I find that she remembers it well. She saw what she thought was a turban wound about the head, and got the impression of color. She wrote the words "not hair" to make this clear. The rest of the comment written at the time was: "See back of head, ear, and swirling scarf tied around head."

XX

I HAVE now given nearly all the 65 drawings which I call "successes," and about half the 155 which I call "partial successes." This, I think, is enough for any purpose. No one can seriously claim that such a set of coincidences could happen by chance, and so it becomes necessary to investigate other possible explanations.

First, a hoax. As covering that point, I prepared a set of affidavits as to the good faith of myself, my wife, her sister, and her sister's husband. These affidavits were all duly signed and witnessed; but friends, reading the manuscript, think they use up space to no purpose, and that the reader will ask no more than the statement that this book is a serious one, and that the manuscript was carefully read by all four of the persons mentioned above, and approved by them as representing the exact truth.

That a group of persons should enter into a conspiracy to perpetrate a hoax is conceivable. Whether or not it is conceivable of the group here quoted is something of which the reader is the judge. But this much is clear: any reader who, having read the above, still suspects us, will not be convinced by further protestations.

How about the possibility of fraud by one person? No one who knows Mary Craig Sinclair would suspect her; but you who do not know her have, naturally, the right to consider such an hypothesis. Can she be one of those women who enjoy being talked about? The broaching of this idea causes her to take the pencil away from her husband, and you now hear her own authentic voice, as follows:

"I happen to be a daughter of that once very living thing, 'the Old South,' and there are certain ideals which are in my blood. The avoidance of publicity is one of them. But even if I had ever had a desire for publicity, it would have been killed by my actual experiences as the wife of a social crusader. My home is besieged by an endless train of persons of every description, who travel over the place, knocking on doors and windows, and insisting upon having a hearing for their various programs for changing the nature

126

of the universe. I have been driven to putting up barriers and fences around my garden, and threatening to flee to the Himalayas, and become a Yogic mistress, or whatever a Yogic 'master' of my sex is called.

"Jack London tried to solve this problem by putting a sign on the front door which read, 'Go to the back door,' and on the back door one which read, 'Go to the front door.' But when I tried this, one seeker of inspiration took his seat halfway between the two doors, and declared that he would remain there the rest of his life, or until his wishes were acceded to. Another hid himself in the swimming-pool, and rose up from its depths to confront me in the dusk, when, as it happened, I was alone on the place, and went out into the garden for a breath of air. A third announced that he had a million dollars to present to my husband in person, and would not be persuaded to depart until my brother invited him to go downtown to supper, and so got him into a car. Having faithfully fed the hungry millionaire, my brother drove him to the police-station, where, after a serious talking-to by the chief, he consented to carry his million dollars away. A fourth introduced himself by mail as having just been released from the psychopathic ward in Los Angeles, and intending to call upon us, for reasons not stated. A fifth announced himself by telephone, as intending to come at once and shoot my husband on sight. Yet another, seven feet tall and broad in proportion, announced that he had a revelation direct from God, and had come to have the manuscript revised. When politely asked as to its nature, he rose up, towering over my none too husky spouse and declaring that no human eye had ever beheld it, and no human eye would ever be permitted to behold it. Such experiences, as a continuing part of a woman's life, do not lead her to seek publicity; they tend rather to develop a persecution complex.

"Speaking seriously, I consider that I have every evidence of the effect of people's thoughts on each other. And my distrust of human nature, in its present stage of evolution, is so great, that the idea of having many persons concentrate their attention on me is an idea from which I shrink. I agree with Richet that the fact of telepathy is one of the most terrifying in existence; and nothing but a deep love of truth has induced me to let this very personal story be told in print."

Next, what about the possibility of unconscious fraud? This also is a question to be frankly met. All students of psychology know that the subconscious mind has dubious morals. One has only to watch his own dreams to discover this. A person in a trance is similar to one talking or walking in sleep, or a drunken man, or one under the influence of a drug. But in this case it must be noted that my wife has never been in a trance. In these mind-reading tests, no matter how intense the "concentration," there is always a part of her mind which knows what she is doing. If you speak to her, she is immediately "all there." When she has her mental pictures, she sits up and makes her drawing, and compares it with mine, and this is a completely conscious act.

Moreover, I point out that a great deal of the most impressive evidence does not depend upon Craig alone. The five drawings with her brother-in-law, figures 1, 16, 17, 18, 19, constitute by themselves evidence of telepathy sufficient to convince any mind which is open to conviction. While it would have been possible for Craig and Bob to hoax Dollie and me, it could certainly not have been done without Bob's connivance. If you suggest that my wife and my brother-in-law may have been fooling me, I reply that there is a still greater mass of evidence which could not have been a hoax without my connivance. When I go into my study alone—a little sun-parlor at the front of a beach-house, with nothing but a couch, a chair and a table—I certainly know that I am alone; and when I make a drawing and hold it before my eyes for five or ten minutes, I certainly know whether any other person is seeing it. This covers the drawings presented as figures 2, 20, and 21, with four others told about in the same series. It seems to me these seven cases by themselves are evidence of telepathy sufficient to convince any open mind.

Furthermore, there are the several score drawings which I made in my study and sealed up in envelopes, taking them to my wife and watching her lay them one by one upon her body and write down more or less accurately what was in them. I certainly know whether I was alone when I made the drawings, and whether I made the contents of the envelopes invisible, and whether my wife had any opportunity to open the envelopes before she made her drawings. Of course, I understand the familiar conjuring trick whereby you open one envelope, and hide it in your palm, and pretend to be describing the next one while really describing the one you have seen. But I would stake my life upon the certainty that my wife knows no sleight-of-hand, and anyhow, I made certain that she did not open the first one; I sat and watched her, and after each test she handed me the envelopes and drawings, one by one—the envelopes having previously been numbered by me. She would turn out the reading-light which was immediately over her head, but there was plenty of light from other parts of the room, enough so that I could look at drawings as they were shown to me. Often these tests were done in the daytime, and then all we did was to pull down the window-shades back of the couch.

It should be obvious that I stand to lose much more than I stand to gain by publishing a book of this sort. Many have urged me not to take the risk. It is the part of prudence not to believe too many new and strange ideas. Some of my Socialist and materialist friends are going to say —without troubling to read what I have written: "Sinclair has gone in for occultism; he is turning into a mystic in his old age." It is true that I am fifty-one, but I think my mind is not entirely gone; and if what I publish here is mysticism, then I do not know how there can be such a thing as science about the human mind.

We have made repeated tests to see what happens; we have written down our observations as we go along; we have presented the evidence carefully and conscientiously, without theories; and what any scientist can do, or ask to have done, more than this, I cannot imagine. Those who throw out these results will not be scientists, but merely another set of dogmatists—of whom new crops are continually springing up, wearing new disguises and new labels. The plain truth is that in science, as in politics and religion, it is a lot easier to believe what you have been taught, than to set out for yourself and ascertain what happens.

Of course the thing would be more convincing if it were done in the presence of strangers. That brings up a question which is bound to be asked, so I will save time by answering it here. The first essential to success in these tests is a state of mind; and at present my wife is a sensitive woman, at the stage of life described as "glandular imbalance." She has never tried these experiments in the presence of a stranger, and has no idea whether she could get the necessary concentration. She learned from her experiments with her sick brother-in-law that the agent can send you pain and fear, as well as chairs and table-forks, and she would certainly not enter lightly into a condition of *rapport* with those whom she did not know and trust.

She insists that the way for you to be really certain is to follow her example. If you sat and watched her do it, you might go away with doubts, as she did after her experiments with Jan. But when you have done it yourself, then you *know*. One reason the thing has not been proven to the public is that people depend on professional mediums, many of whom are deliberate and conscious cheats. Others are vain and temperamental, difficult to manage; and research is hindered by their instability. That is why Craig set to work and learned to do it, and she believes that others can do the same, if they have the desire and the patience.

XXI

THE next thing is to carry out our promise and tell you the technique. My wife has, among her notes, a mass of writing on this subject in the form of instructions to Bob, and others who were interested. I tried to condense it, but found I could not satisfy her, and in the end I realized that her point of view is correct. No one objects to repetition of phrases in a legal document, where the one essential is precision; and the same thing applies to descriptions of these complicated mental processes. This was the most difficult writing task she ever undertook, and the reason lies in its newness, and the complexity of the mind itself.

If you want to learn the art of conscious mind-reading, this will tell you how; and if you don't want to learn it, you can easily skip this section of the book. Here is Craig's statement:

"The first thing you have to do is to learn the trick of undivided attention, or concentration. By these terms I mean something quite different from what is ordinarily meant. One 'concentrates' on writing a chapter in a book, or on solving a problem in mathematics; but this is a complicated process of dividing one's attention, giving it to one detail after another, judging, balancing, making decisions. The kind of concentration I mean is putting the attention on *one* object, or one *uncomplicated* thought, such as joy, or peace, and holding it there steadily. It isn't thinking; it is inhibiting thought, except for one thought, or one object in thought.

"You have to inhibit the impulse to think things about the object, to examine it, or appraise it, or to allow memory-trains to attach themselves to it. The average person has never heard of such a form of concentration, and so has to learn how to do it. Simultaneously, he must learn to relax, for strangely enough, a part of concentration is complete relaxation.

"There seems to be a contradiction here, in the idea of simultaneous concentration and relaxation. I do not know whether this is due to a contradiction in the nature of the mind itself, or to our misunderstanding of its nature. Perhaps we each have several mental entities, or minds, and one of these can sleep (be blankly unconscious), while another supervises the situation, maintaining the first one's state of unconsciousness for a desired period, and then presenting to it some thought or picture agreed on in advance, thus restoring it to consciousness.

"Anyway, it is possible to be unconscious and conscious at the same time! Almost every one has had the experience of knowing, while asleep, that he is having a bad dream and must awaken himself from it. Certainly some conscious entity is watching the dream, and knowing it is a dream; and yet the sleeper is 'unconscious.' Or perhaps there is no such thing as complete relaxation—until death.

"All I can say is this: when I practice this art which I have learned, with my mind concentrated on one simple thing, it is a relaxation as restful, as seemingly 'complete,' as when I am in that state called normal sleep. The attention is not allowed to be on the sensations of the body, or on anything but the one thing it is deliberately 'concentrated' on.

"Undivided concentration, then, means, for purposes of this experiment, a state of complete relaxation, under specified control.

To concentrate in this undivided way you first give yourself a 'suggestion' to the effect that you will relax your mind and your body, making the body insensitive and the mind a blank, and yet reserving power to 'break' the concentration in a short time. By making the body insensitive I mean simply to relax completely your mental hold of, or awareness of, all bodily sensation. After giving yourself this suggestion a few times, you proceed to relax both body and mind. Relax all mental interest in everything in the environment; inhibit all thoughts which try to wander into consciousness from the subconsciousness, or from wherever else thoughts come. This is clearly a more thorough affair than 'just relaxing.'

"Also, there is something else to it—the power of supervising the condition. You succeed presently in establishing a blank state of consciousness, yet you have the power to become instantly conscious, also; to realize when you are about to go into a state of sleep, in which you have not the power of instantly returning to consciousness. Also, you control, to a certain degree, what is to be presented to consciousness when you are ready to become conscious. For example, you want a message from the person who is sending you a message; you do not want a train of subconscious 'day dreams.'

"All this is work; and so far, it is a bore. But when you have learned to do it, it is an art worth knowing. You can use it, not only for such experiments as telepathy and clairvoyance, but for improving your bodily health. To relax thoroughly several times each day while holding on to a suggestion previously 'planted' in the subconsciousness is more beneficial to health than any other one measure I know.

"The way to relax is to 'let go.' 'Let go' of every tense muscle, every tense spot, in the body. Pain is tension. Pain can be inhibited by suggestion *followed by complete relaxation*. Drop your body, a dead-weight, from your conscious mind. Make your conscious mind a blank. It is the mind, conscious or subconscious, which holds the body tense. Give to the subconsciousness the suggestion of concentrating on one idea, and then completely relax consciousness. To make the conscious mind a blank it is necessary to 'let go' of the body; just as to 'let go' of the body requires 'letting

132

go' of consciousness of the body. If, after you have practiced 'letting go' of the body, you find that your mind is not a blank, then you have not succeeded in getting your body rid of all tension. Work at it until you can let both mind and body relax completely.

"It may help you to start as follows: Relax the body as completely as possible. Then visualize a rose, or a violet—some pleasant, familiar thing which does not arouse emotional memory-trains. Gaze steadily, peacefully, at the chosen object—think only of it—try not to let any memories it may arouse enter your mind. Keep attention steady, just seeing the color, or the shape of the flower and nothing else. Do not think things about the flower. Just look at it. Select one thing about it to concentrate on, such as its shape, or its color, or the two combined in a visual image: 'pink and round.'

"If you find that you are made nervous by this effort, it is apt to be due to the fact that you are thinking things. Maybe the object you have chosen has some buried memories associated with it—something which arouses unconscious memories of past unhappy events Roses may suggest a lost sweetheart, or a vanished garden where you once were happy and to which you long to return. If so, select some other flower to concentrate on. Flowers are usually the most restful, the things which are not so apt to be involved with distressing experiences. A bottle of ink might suggest the strain of mental work, a spoon might suggest medicine, So, find a peace-inspiring object to look at. When you have found it, just look at it, with undivided attention.

"If you succeed in doing this, you will find it hard not to drop asleep. But you must distinguish between this and the state you are to maintain. If you drop asleep, the sleep will be what is called auto-hypnotic sleep, and after you have learned to induce it, you will be able to concentrate on an idea, instead of the rose, and to carry this idea into the sleep with you as the idea to dominate the subconsciousness while you sleep. This idea, taken with you into sleep in this way, will often act in the subconsciousness with the same power as the idea suggested by a hypnotist. If you have ever seen hypnotism, you will know what this means. You can learn to carry an idea of the restoration of health into this auto-hypnotic sleep, to act powerfully during sleep. Of course this curative effect is not always achieved. Any idea introduced into the subconsciousness may meet a counter-suggestion which, if you are ill, already exists in the subconsciousness, and a conflict may ensue. Thus, time and perseverance may be necessary to success.

"But this is another matter, and not the state for telepathy—in which you must avoid dropping into a sleep. After you have practiced the exercise of concentrating on a flower—and avoiding sleep—you will be able to concentrate on holding the peculiar blank state of mind which must be achieved if you are to make successful experiments in telepathy. There may be strain to start with, but it is getting rid of strain, both physical and mental, which constitutes relaxation, or blankness, of the conscious mind. Practice will teach you what this state is, and after a while you can achieve it without strain.

"The next step: ask some one to draw a half-dozen simple designs for you on cards, or on slips of paper, and to fold them so that you cannot see the contents. They should be folded separately, so that you can handle one at a time. Place them on a table, or chair, beside your couch, or bed, in easy reach of your hand, so that you can pick them up, one at a time, while you are stretched out on the bed, or couch, beside them. It is best at first to experiment in the dark, or at least in a dimly lit room, as light stimulates the eyes and interferes with relaxation. If you experiment at night, have a table lamp within easy reach, so that you can turn the light off and on for each experiment without too much exertion, as you must keep your body and mind as passive as possible for these experiments. If you have no reading light near, use a candle. You must have also a writing pad and pencil beside you.

"After you have placed the drawings on the table, turn off the light and stretch your body full length on the couch. Close your eyes and relax your body. Relax completely. Make the mind a complete blank and hold it blank. Do not think of anything. Thoughts will come. Inhibit them. Refuse to think. Do this for several moments. It is essential to induce a passive state of mind and body. If the mind is not passive, it feels body sensations. If the body is not relaxed, its sensations interfere with the necessary mental passivity. Each reacts on the other.

134

"The next step, after having turned off the light and closed your eyes and relaxed mind and body full length on the couch, is to reach for the top drawing of the pile on the table. Hold it in your hand over your solar plexus. Hold it easily, without clutching it. Now, completely relaxed, hold your mind a blank again. Hold it so for a few moments, then give the mental order to the unconscious mind to tell you what is on the paper you hold in your hand. Keep the eyes closed and the body relaxed, and give the order silently, and with as little mental exertion as possible.

"However, it is necessary to give it clearly and positively, that is, with concentration on it. Say to the unconscious mind, 'I want the picture which is on this card, or paper, presented to my consciousness.' Say this with your mind concentrated on what you are saying. Repeat, as if talking directly to another self: 'I want to see what is on *this* card.' Then relax into blankness again and hold blankness a few moments, then try gently, without straining, to see whatever forms may appear on the void into which you look with closed eyes. Do not try to conjure up something to see; just wait expectantly and let something come.

"My experience is that fragments of forms appear first. For example, a curved line, or a straight one, or two lines of a triangle. But sometimes the complete object appears; swiftly, lightly, dimly-drawn, as on a moving picture film. These mental visions appear and disappear with lightning rapidity, never standing still unless quickly fixed by a deliberate effort of consciousness. They are never in heavy lines, but as if sketched delicately, in a slightly deeper shade of gray than that of the mental canvas. A person not used to such experiments may at first fail to observe them on the gray background of the mind, on which they appear and disappear so swiftly. Sometimes they are so vague that one gets only a notion of how they look before they vanish. Then one must 'recall' this first vision. Recall it by conscious effort, which is not the same thing as the method of passive waiting by which the vision was first induced. Instead, it is as if one had seen with open eyes a fragment of a real picture, and now closes his eyes and looks at the *memory* of it and tries to 'see' it clearly.

"It is necessary to recall this vision and make note of it, so as not to forget it. One is sure to forget it—indeed it is his duty to do so—in the process of the next step, which is one of blankness again. This blankness is, of course, a deliberate putting out of the conscious mind of all pictures, including the one just visioned. One must now order the subconscious not to present it to the conscious mind's picture-film again unless it is the right picture, *i.e.*, the one drawn on the card which is held in hand. Make the conscious mind blank again for a brief space. Then look again on the gray canvas of mind for a vision. This is to test whether the first vision came from subconscious guessing, or whether it came from the deeper mind— from some other source than that of the subconscious, which is so apt to offer a 'guess,' or false picture.

"Do this whole performance two or three times, and if the first vision persists in coming back, accept it. As soon as you have accepted it—that is, decided that this is the correct vision —turn on the light, and without looking at the card, or paper, which contains the real picture, pick up the writing pad and pencil and make a sketch of every detail of the vision-picture. This is a nuisance, as it interrupts concentration and the desired passivity. But it is absolutely necessary to record the vision in every detail, before one looks at the real picture, the one on the card he has been holding in hand. If one does not make a record of his vision in advance of looking at the card picture, he is certain to forget at least some part of it—maybe something which is essential. Worse yet, he is apt to fool himself; the mind is given to self-deception. As soon as it sees the real drawing, it not only forgets the vision, but it is apt to imagine that it visioned the picture it now sees on the card, which may or may not be true. Imagination is a far more active function than the average person realizes. This conscious-subconscious mind is 'a liar,' a weaver of fiction. It is the dream-mind, and also it is the mind of memory trains.

"Do not omit fragments which seem to be out of place in a picture. These fragments may be the real things. If in doubt as to what the object of your vision is, do not try to guess. But if you have a 'hunch' that something you have seen is connected somehow with a watch, for example, or with an automobile, make a note of this 'hunch.' I use this popular word to indicate a real presentation from some true source, something deeper and more dependable than our own subconscious minds. I call this the 'deep mind' in order to have a name for it. I do not know what it is, of course—I am only judging from the behavior of the phenomena.

"Do not fail to record what seems to be a stray fragment, for it may be a perfect vision of some portion of the real picture. Record everything, and then later you can compare it carefully with the real drawing. Of course, do not be fantastic in your conclusions. Do not think you have gotten a correct vision of an automobile because you saw a circle which resembled a wheel. However, I once saw a circle and *felt* that it was an automobile wheel—felt it so vividly that I became overwhelmed with curiosity to see if my 'feeling' was correct, and forthwith turned on the light and examined the real picture in my hand. I found that it was indeed the wheel of an automobile. But I do not do this kind of thing unless I have a very decided 'hunch,' as it tends to lead back to the natural impulse of the mind to 'guess'—and guessing is one of the things one has to strive to avoid. To a certain extent, one comes to know a difference between a guess and a 'hunch.'

"The details of this technique are not to be taken as trifles. The whole issue of success or failure depends on them. At least, this is so in my case. Perhaps a spontaneous sensitive, or one who has a better method, has no such difficulties. I am just an average conscious-minded person, who set out deliberately to find a way to test this tremendously important question of telepathy and clairvoyance, without having to depend on a 'medium,' who might be fooling himself, or me. It was by this method of careful attention to a technique of details that I have found it possible to get telepathic messages and to see pictures on hidden cards, and symbolic pictures of the contents of books.

"This technique takes time, and patience, and training in the art of concentration. But this patience is in itself an excellent thing to learn, especially for nervous and sick people. The uses of mental concentration are too various and tremendously beneficial to enumerate here. The average person has almost no power of concentration, as he will quickly discover by trying to hold his undivided attention on one simple object, such as a rose, or a bottle of ink, for just a few minutes. He will find that a thousand thoughts, usually association trains connected with the rose, or the ink, will appear on his mental canvas, interrupting his

137

concentration. He will find that his mind behaves exactly like a moving-picture film, or a fireworks display. It is the division of attention that uses up energy, if I am not mistaken.

"Of course this technique is not 'original.' I got it by selecting from hints here and there in my reading, and from my general study and observation of the behavior of the mind.

"Among the difficulties to be overcome—and this is one which is easily detected—is the appearing of visions of objects one has observed in the environment just before closing the eyes. When I close my eyes to make the next test, I invariably find that the last picture, and my own drawing of it, and also the electric light bulb which I have lighted in order to see the last picture—all these immediately appear on the horizon of my mind. It often takes quite a while to banish these memory-ghosts. And sometimes it is a mistake to banish them, as the picture you hold in your hand may be quite similar to the preceding one. If, therefore, a picture resembling the preceding continues obstinately to represent itself, I usually accept it, and often find that the preceding and present cards contain similar pictures.

"Another difficulty is the way things sometimes appear in fragments, or sections, of the whole picture. A straight line may appear, and it may be either only a portion of the whole, or it may be all there is on the card. Then I have to resist the efforts of my imagination to speculate as to what object this fragment may be part of. For instance, I see a series of points, and have the impulse to 'guess' a star. I must say no to this guess-work, unless the indescribable 'hunch' feeling assures me it is a star. I must tell myself it may be indeed a part of a star, but, on the other hand, it may be a complete picture of the drawing in hand, perhaps the letter W, or M, or it may be a part of a pennant, or what not. Then I must start over, and hold blank a while. Then repeat the request to the deep mind for the true picture. Now I may get a more complete picture, or maybe this fragment reappears alone, or maybe it repeats itself upside-down, or doubled up in most any way.

138

"I start all over once more and now I may get a series of fragments which follow each other and jump together as do the comic cartoons which are drawn on the screen with pen and ink. For instance, two points appear, then another appears separately and jumps to the first two, and joins up with them, then two more. The result is a star, and this may be the true picture. It usually is. But sometimes this is the subconscious mind, or perhaps the conscious, trying to finish the object as it has 'guessed' it should be. This error of allowing the conscious or the subconscious mind to finish the object is one to be most careful about. As one experiments, he realizes more and more that these two minds, the conscious and the subconscious, are really one, subconsciousness being only a disorderly store-house of memories. The third, or 'deep mind' is apparently the one which gives us our psychic phenomena. Again I say, I do not know what this 'deep mind' is; I use the words merely to have a name for that 'other thing' which brings the message.

"The conscious mind, combined with the subconscious, not only wants to finish the picture, but decides sometimes to eliminate a detail which does not belong to what it has guessed should be there. For example, I will discuss the drawings which have been given as figures 35, 35a, in this book. I 'visioned' what looked like a figure 5, except that at the top where there should be a small vertical line projecting toward the right, there was a flare of very long lines converging at one end. I consciously decided that the long lines were an exaggeration and multiplication of what should properly be at the top of a five, and that I should not accept them. Here was conscious mind making a false decision. But by obeying the rules I had laid down in advance, I was saved from this error of consciousness. I closed my eyes, gave a call for the true picture, and the lines appeared again, so I included them in my drawing. When I opened the envelope and looked at the picture inside, it was an oil derrick. So the flare of long lines was the real thing, while the figure 5 was the interloper—at least, so I now consciously decided. I thought that the figure 5 and the flare of lines were entirely separate mental images, one following the other so rapidly that they appeared to belong together.

"But again my conscious decision was in error. Several hours later, after I had put the whole matter out of my mind and had been attending to household duties, I suddenly remembered the paper

139

jacket of a German edition of my husband's novel, 'Oil,' which was on a shelf in the next room to the one in which I had made my experiments. Why did I suddenly remember this book? I had not noticed it for a long time —its jacket drawings were out of sight, as the book was wedged between many others on the book shelves in an inconspicuous place in the room. On one side of the jacket of this book was a picture of three oil derricks; on the other side was a large dollar mark, almost covering one entire side of the book. I had seen this jacket, had indeed taken special notice of it, at the time of its arrival from Germany. So here seems to have been a clear case of the subconscious mind at work during my experiment, adding to my true vision of an oil derrick, the subconsciously remembered dollar mark which looked like a figure 5, partly hidden by the oil derrick in my vision. Here was a grand mix-up of the false guesses of consciousness and subconsciousness, and the true presentations from the 'deep mind.'

"But this was not the end. This confusion in regard to the dollar mark went forward, in memory-trains to two other experiments. Several days later, I was trying a new set of drawings, and one of them caused in my mind a vision of the capital letter S. Instantly, two parallel straight lines crossed it, turning it into a dollar mark: $. Then it became an S again without the lines. Then the lines came back. This strange behavior of my vision continued. I was in a quandary as to which to accept, the S or the $. Then there appeared an old-fashioned money-bag, such as I used to see in my father's bank as a child, full of small coins. It took its place in the vision beside the dollar mark. I decided with the usual erroneous consciousness that this money-bag was a hint from my real mind, so I accepted the dollar mark as correct. But it turned out not to be. When I looked at the drawing in hand it was a letter S. My subconsciousness had supplied the money-bag, and the two parallel lines.

"Several days later, in a vision with a third set of drawings, I saw a letter S, and then at once the bag of small change appeared, but there were no parallel lines on the S. This time the real drawing was a dollar mark! So, my subconsciousness, as soon as the dollar mark had appeared in subconsciousness, had meddled again; it had remembered the last experiment and the scolding I had given it for its guess work, so it now subtracted the parallel lines from the new

140

vision to make it correct, according to the last experiment. It had remembered the last experiment only, forgetting the first one, of the oil derrick, just as I had ordered it to do on the occasion of the second experiment. So, it subtracted the two parallel lines, but it added the remembered bag of money, which I had included in my scolding. From this kind of interference by the subconsciousness, I realized that it is indeed no simple matter to get things into consciousness from the 'deep mind' without guesses and additions and subtractions made by the subconsciousness. Why the subconscious should meddle, I do not know. But it does. Its behavior is exactly like that of the conscious mind, which is also prone to guessing. All this sounds fantastic—to any one who has not studied his mind. But I tell you how it seems to me.

"Maybe everything comes from the subconscious. Maybe there is no 'deep mind.' Maybe the subconscious gets its knowledge of what is on the drawing directly from the drawing, and is merely blundering around, adding details by guess-work to what it has seen incompletely. But I think that these experiments prove that this is not the case. I think a study of them shows that a true vision comes into the subconsciousness, not directly from the drawing, but from another mind which has some means of knowing, and sending to consciousness via the subconsciousness whatever I ask it for. Of course I cannot attempt to prove this here. It was one of the questions to which I was seeking an answer, and the result seems to point to the existence of a deeper mind, showing how its behavior is quite different from that of the subconscious.

"I wanted to find out if the true vision could in any way be distinguished from 'imagination,' or these busy guesses of the subconsciousness. To help myself in this matter, I first made an examination of exactly how these guesses come. I said to myself: every thought that ever comes to consciousness, excepting those due to direct outside stimulation, may proceed from some deeper source, and by subconscious memory-trains attaching to them, appear to be the work of subconsciousness. So I shut my eyes and made my mind blank, without calling on my mind to present any definite thing. I had no drawing in my hand. After a brief space of blankness, I relaxed the enforced blankness and waited, dreamily, for what might come. A picture soon came, with a whole memory-train. First a girl in a large garden hat, then a garden path and flowers bordering it, then a spade, a wheelbarrow, and so on—things associated in my memory with a girl in a garden hat. As to where the girl in the hat came from, I know not. As to why she should come instead of any other of billions of things seen by me during my life, I know not. I had not asked my mind for her. The question of why she came is interesting.

"But it was easy to account for the other things—the association-train. I learned from this experiment, and several repetitions of it, that something always came—a girl, or a steamship, or the fact that I had not attended to some household duty, or what not—and a train of associated ideas followed. I learned, in a more or less vague way, how these things behaved, and how I *felt* about them. This enabled me to notice, when later I got a true vision, that there was a difference between the way this true vision came and the way the 'idle' visions came. When the true visions came, there usually came with them a 'something' which I call a 'hunch.' There was, of course, always in my consciousness the question: is this the right thing, or not? When the true vision came, this question seemed to receive an answer, 'yes,' as if some intelligent entity was directly informing me.

"This was not always the case. At times no answer came, or at least, if it came, it was obscured by guesses. But usually it did, after I had watched for it, and a sort of thrill of triumph came with it, quite different from the quiet way in which the money-bag had appeared in answer to my uncertainty. The subconscious answers questions, and its answers are always false; its answers come quietly, like a thief in the night. But the 'other' mind, the 'deep mind' answers questions, too, and these answers come, not quietly, but as if by 'inspiration,' whatever that is—with a rustling of wings, with gladness and conviction. These two minds seem different from each other. One lies and rambles; the other sings, and is truthful.

"But do not misunderstand me. I am not a religious convert. I am searching for knowledge, and recording what I find. Others on this search may have found these same things, but the conclusions they have drawn may not turn out to be the ones I shall draw.

"One or two other things of interest should perhaps be mentioned. First, I found that, in doing a series of several drawings, the percentage of successes was higher in the first three attempts. Then there began to be failures, alternating with successes. This may have been due to the fact that the memory-pictures of these first three experiments now constituted a difficulty. So much attention had to be given to inhibiting these memory-pictures, and in deciding whether or not they were to be inhibited. Or it may be due to some other cause, such as fatigue or boredom.

"The second detail is that during the earliest experiments, I developed a headache. I think this was due to the fact that I strained my closed eyes trying to see with them. I mean, of course, trying to see a vision, not the card in my hand. Using the eyes to see with is a habit, and habits are not easily overcome. I soon learned not to use my eyes, at least not in a strained way, and this was the end of the headaches. However, this use of the eyes in telepathy may perhaps mean more than a mere habit. The mental canvas on which these 'visions' are projected seems to be spread in the eyes, and it is the eyes which seem to see them—despite the fact that the room may be dark, the eyes closed, and the drawing on the paper be wrapped in thick covering and not within normal range of the eyes. But this may be due to the habit of associating all pictures with your eyes."

XXII

So much for the art of voluntary mind-reading. In conclusion I attempt to say a few words about what these phenomena mean, and how they come about.

This attempt involves me in a verbal duel with my wife, which lasts into the small hours of morning. It involves the everlasting debate between the vitalists and the mechanists, which had best be left to Dr. Watson and Professor McDougall, and the others who are no more able than I am to look at the neurons of the brain in action, to see what happens. But I insist that until Craig and Dr. Watson, Professor Eddington and Mrs. Eddy have found out positively whether the universe is all mind or all matter, I must go on speaking in the old-fashioned way, as if there were two worlds, the physical and the mental, two sets of phenomena which interact one upon the other continuously, even though the manner of this happening is beyond comprehension.

With this much apology, I obtain permission to put forth my humble guess as to the part played by mental concentration in the causing of telepathy, clairvoyance, and trance phenomena. It seems to me that the process of intense concentration may cause the nervous energy, or brain energy, whatever it is, to be withdrawn from some of the brain centers and transferred to others; and it may be this displacement and disturbance of balance which accounts for such phenomena as catalepsy, automatism, and somnambulism. Portions of the mind which are ordinarily below the level of consciousness are raised to more intense forms of activity. New levels of mind are tapped, new "personalities" or faculties are brought into action, and persons under hypnotism develop mental powers they do not consciously possess.

That it is intense concentration upon one suggestion—the narrowing of the attention to one focus—which produces the cataleptic trance is something which my wife set out to prove, and by going close to the border-line she feels that she did prove it. The rigidity began at the extremities and crept rapidly over the body. In spite of my protests, Craig insisted that she was going the whole way, and asked me to stand by and make some tests. I was to wait three minutes, and then lift her up by the feet. I did so, and found an extraordinary thing—the body was perfectly rigid, like a log of wood, except at the neck! When I lifted her by her feet, the neck bent, so that the head remained on the pillow, while the feet were raised at least a yard in the air. Later, when Craig had relaxed, she told me that she had known what was happening; there had been one point of consciousness left, and she had the belief that she could let that go in another moment, but was afraid to do so, because she might not come out again. For an instant, she had felt that strange terror one feels at the moment he ceases to struggle against the fumes of gas or ether, and plunges into oblivion. The difference is that, in the case of gas or ether, one cannot hold on to consciousness; but in the case of the cataleptic state, he can recall his receding consciousness. Craig, of course, had not concentrated with complete attention to one idea; one portion of her mind was concentrated upon achieving rigidity, while another was watching and protesting against oblivion.

Dr. Morton Prince wrote to Craig: "You are playing with powerful and dangerous forces." And so she dropped this form of experiment. But more should be known about these trances, which often occur spontaneously, and can be caused by fear—that is to say, an intense concentration on the idea of escape from danger, which produces a tension amounting to paralysis. In such cases there are a number of new dangers; one being that some doctor will try to restore you with drugs and wrong suggestions. Every suggestion of fear on the part of the onlookers must be avoided in case of trances, for the subconscious mind of the victim hears every word, and believes it; also telepathy has to be remembered. One must not only speak quietly and firmly, repeating that everything is all right, and that the person will come out safely; one must also *think* this. The trance may last a long time, but keep calm and sure of success, and keep the doctor and the undertaker away. The condition of catalepsy is more common than is realized, and it is unpleasant to think how many persons are embalmed while in this condition.

All this sounds disturbing, but it has nothing to do with our telepathy experiments, in which the state of concentration is not one of tension accompanied by the suggestion of rigidity, or of fear, but on the contrary is a state of relaxation, accompanied by the suggestion of control, or supervision. This matter of supervision has been carefully set forth by Craig in her statement. It is one of the mind's great mysteries: how, while thinking about nothing, you can not only remember to give a suggestion, but can also act upon it. Craig insists that we have three minds.; and she has in this the backing of William McDougall, who is probably the "dean" of American psychologists, now that Morton Prince is dead. Professor McDougall talks about the various "monads" of the mind; so let us say that one "monad" gives an order to a second "monad" to become blank, after it has given an order to a third to present to the first a picture.

The psychic Jan gives such "autosuggestions" to himself when he goes into a trance, and tells his trance mind to bring him out at a certain moment. How that trance mind can measure time as exactly

145

as a clock is another of the mysteries; but that it happens is beyond doubt. My wife took Jan to a group of scientists in Boston, and several of them held watches and expressed their surprise at what Jan was able to do. It is obvious that when the psychic lets himself be buried six feet under the ground in an ordinary pine-wood coffin, he is staking his life upon his certainty that he will not come out of the state of lethargy until after he has been dug up.

He also stakes it upon the hope that the physicians who have the test in charge will have sufficient sense to realize the importance of having him dug out at the time agreed. In one case they were several minutes late, and Jan nearly suffocated. I never saw one of these burials, because Craig obtained his promise not to do them after she knew him; but I have talked with several physicians who watched and directed all the details, and I have a moving-picture film of one.

XXIII

MENTION telepathy in company, and almost every one has a story to tell. You can find a clairvoyant to tell you about yourself for a dollar—and maybe she is a fraud, but then again, maybe she is a person with a gift, which she does not understand, and the police throw her into jail because they don't understand it either. I am sorry if I aid the mass of fraud which I know exists in this field, but there is no power of man, which may not and will not be abused. The person who invented high explosives and made possible great tunnels and bridges, also made possible the destruction of the Louvain library. The person who makes a dynamo may electrocute himself.

In spite of all fraud, I am convinced that there are thousands of genuine clairvoyants and psychics. My friend Will Irwin told me recently how he spent a year or so collecting material and writing an exposure of fraud, "The Medium Game," published in *Collier's Weekly* some twenty years ago. At the end of his labors he went, on sudden impulse, into a "parlor" on Sixth Avenue, a cheap neighborhood of New York, and a fat old woman in a greasy wrapper took his dollar, and held his hand in hers, and told him things which he believed were known to no human being but Will Irwin.

"What is the use of it?" some will ask. I reply with another question: "What was the use of the lightning which Franklin brought down from the clouds on his kite-string?" No use that Franklin ever knew; yet to-day we make his lightning turn the wheels of industry, and move great railroad systems, and light a hundred million homes, and spread jazz music and cigarette advertising thousands of miles in every direction. It is an axiom of the scientist that every scrap of knowledge will be put to use sooner or later; get it, and let the uses wait. The discovery of the cause of bubonic plague was made possible because some foolish-minded entomologist had thought it worth-while to collect information about the fleas which prey upon the bodies of rats and ground squirrels.

I know a certain Wall Street operator who employed a "psychic" to sit in at his business conferences, and tell him if the other fellow was honest. I believe it didn't work very well; perhaps the circumstances were not favorable to concentration. Needless to say, Craig and I have no interest in such uses to be made of our knowledge. What telepathy means to my wife is this: it seems to indicate a common substratum of mind, underlying our individual minds, and which we can learn to tap. Figure the conscious mind as a tree, and the subconscious mind as the roots of that tree: then what of the earth in which the tree grows, and from which it derives its sustenance? What currents run through that earth, affecting all the trees of the forest? If one tree falls, the earth is shaken—and may not the other trees feel the impulse?

In other words, we are apparently getting hints of a cosmic consciousness, or cosmic unconsciousness: some kind of mind stuff which is common to us all, and which we can bring into our individual consciousness. Why is it not sensible to think that there may be a universal mind-stuff, just as there is a universal body-stuff, of which we are made, and to which we return?

When Craig orders her mind, or some portion of it, or faculty of it, to get what is in Bob's mind, while Bob is forty miles away—and when her mind does that, what are we to picture as happening? If I am correct in my guess, that mind and body are two aspects of one reality, then we shall find some physical form of energy being manifested, just as we do when we communicate by sound waves. The human brain is a storage battery, capable of sending impulses over the nerves. Why may it not be capable of sending impulses by means of some other medium, known or unknown? Why may there not be such a thing as brain radio?

Certainly we know this, that every particle of energy in the universe affects to some slight extent every other particle. The problem of detecting such energy is merely one of getting a sufficiently sensitive device. Who can say that our thoughts are not causing vibrations? Who can set a limit to the distance they may travel, or to the receiving powers of another brain, in some way or other attuned thereto? Any truly scientific person will admit that this is a possibility, and that it is purely a question of experimenting, to find out if it does happen, and how.

Again, consider the problem of clairvoyance, suggested by Craig's ability to tell what is inside a book she holds in her hand without seeing it, or to reproduce drawings when no human mind knows what drawing she holds. How are we to figure that as happening? Shall we say that brain vibrations affect material things such as paper, and leave impressions which endure for a long time, possibly forever? Can these affect another brain, as in the case of a bit of radium giving off emanations? It seems to me correct to say that, theoretically, it is inevitable. Every particle of energy that has ever been manifested in the universe goes on producing its effects somewhere, somehow, and the universe is forever different because of that happening. The soil of Britain is still shaking with the tramp of Cæsar's legions, two thousand years old. Who can say that some day we may not have instruments sensitive enough to detect such traces of energy? On the very day that I am reading the galley proofs of this book, I find in my morning paper an Associated Press dispatch, from which I clip a few paragraphs.

"A fundamental discovery in photography that takes the 'pictures' directly on cold, hard untreated metal without the usual photographer's medium of a sensitized plate was made public to-night at Cornell University. It reveals that seemingly impervious

148

metal records on its surface unseen impressions from streams of electrons and that these marks can be brought into visibility by the right kind of a 'developer,' exactly as photographic images are brought out on sensitized paper. . . .

"While studying sensitivity of photographic plates to electron rays it suddenly was realized that polished metal surfaces might be able to pick up impressions of these beams, and when tests were made they showed that not only could such records be made on metals, but the amazing fact appeared that some metals are almost as sensitive as photographic film, and for very low velocity electrons much more sensitive. . . .

"This young physicist one day was looking at the rough spots produced on the metal target of an X-ray tube by electron bombardment. Such spots are commonplace, familiar sights to laboratory workers. It occurred to Dr. Carr that perhaps long before the electrons produced the rough place they made an invisible impression, which might be 'developed' in the same manner that the still invisible image on a photo is brought out by putting it into a developing bath. Carr shot the electron rays at gold plates and developed them with mercury vapor, he shot them at silver and developed with iodine, he used hydrochloric acid to develop zinc plates and iodine to develop copper."

And now, if X-rays leave a permanent record on metal, why might not brain-rays, or thought-rays, leave a record upon a piece of paper? Why might not such energies be reflected back to another brain, as light is reflected by a mirror? Or perhaps the record might stay as some other form of energy, turned back into brain-rays or thought-rays by the percipient. We are familiar with this in the telephone, where sound vibrations are turned into electrical vibrations, and in this form transported across a continent and under an ocean, and then turned back into sound vibrations once again.

That mental activities do leave some kind of record on matter seems certain; at any rate, it is the basic concept of the materialistic psychologist. For what is memory, to the materialist, but some kind of record upon brain cells? He compares these cells

149

to photoelectric cells, and imagines a lot of stored up records, which we can consult. If now it should be found that such memory records are impressed, not merely upon living brain cells, but upon the molecules or electrons which compose any form of matter, what would be so incredible about that?

I have gone this far, in the effort to meet my materialist friends halfway. For my part, I have no metaphysics; I am content to say that I do not know what matter is, nor what mind is, nor how they interact. If you want to realize the inadequacies of the materialistic dogma, so far as concerns this special field, you may consult the work of Dr. Rudolph Tischner, a qualified scientist of Germany, whose book, "Telepathy and Clairvoyance," is published in translation by Harcourt, Brace and Company. The last chapter, called "Theory," deals with the suggested explanations in more detail than I have the space for here.

XXIV

April 21, 1929. I am over at the office fixing up this manuscript to send to the publisher; and just as I have it nicely wrapped, it has to be opened again—for this is what has happened. Craig, with her anxiety complex, has had this thought: "Here is Upton committing himself in this public way, on a subject about which people know so little and suspect so much; and suppose this faculty, whatever it is, should be gone in these last few weeks, while I have been fussing over spring housecleaning! Suppose I should find I can never do it again!"

She has to make sure all over again. She has in her desk a fat envelope marked: "To try." A lot of old drawings, left-overs from different series that she has tried and failed on during the past several months; some that she herself has drawn for friends; some that she was interrupted while doing—a job lot, in short. She does not know how many, as she has stuck them in from time to time, and never looked into the envelope; but it is well filled. Now she takes out some drawings, with averted eyes, and lies down and tries them. The house is quiet, a good opportunity, so she does nine drawings, and there is only one complete failure in the lot.

One is a marvel—as good as any. It is a drawing I had made, a donkey's head and neck, with a wide collar. Craig writes: "Cow's head in 'stock'"—a "stock" being in Mississippi a wooden yoke made to keep cattle from jumping fences. She draws the head of the so-called "cow" and the "stock"; it is a perfect donkey's head, facing just as mine does.

And then there is a duck, about to eat a snail. Such a jolly duck, and such a wheely snail shell! Craig has made this drawing to amuse the little daughter of Bob and Dolly, who had a pet duck, called "Mary Ann," fed on snails. Craig made this drawing several months ago, to let the child "concentrate" on, and try telepathy like the grown-ups. And now, with this drawing under her hand, Craig writes: "See wheels. Think of children. Has to do with children." The drawing of the snail shell is plainly a lot of "wheels."

Now, of course, Craig had previously seen every one of these drawings, and so they were all in her subconscious mind. But these drawings had never been seen by her at the same time. They were put into the envelope, some at one time, some at another. Now she has taken out a few at random. What a jumble for any subconscious mind to keep track of! How is Craig's mind to know which drawings she has taken out, and which one she is holding under her hand?

Again we have something more than telepathy. For no human mind knows what drawings she has taken from that envelope. No human mind but her own even knows that she is trying an experiment. Either there is some superhuman mind, or else there is something that comes from the drawings, some way of "seeing," other than the way we know and use all the time. Make what you can of this, but don't laugh at it, for most certainly it happens.

XXV

October, 1929. At my wife's insistence, I have held up this book for six months, in order to think it over, and have the manuscript read by friends whose opinions we value. A score or more have read it, and made various suggestions, many of which I have accepted.

Some of the reactions of these friends may be of interest to the reader.

The news that I was taking up "psychic" matters brought me letters both of curiosity and protest. My friend Isaac Goldberg of Boston reported the matter in the Haldeman-Julius publications under the title: "Sinclair Goes Spooky." I hope that when he has read this book, he will find another adjective. My friends, both radical and respectable, must realize that I have dealt here with facts, in as patient and thorough a manner as I have ever done in my life. It is foolish to be convinced without evidence, but it is equally foolish to refuse to be convinced by real evidence.

There came to me a letter of warning from a good comrade, T. H. Bell of Los Angeles, an elderly Scotchman who has grown up in the revolutionary movement, and known the old fighters of the days when I was a child. He begged me not to jeopardize my reputation; so I thought he would be a good test for the manuscript, and asked him to read it. Some of his suggestions I accepted, and the work is the better for them. But Comrade Bell was not able to believe that Craig's drawings could have come by telepathy, for the reason that it would mean that he was "abandoning the fundamental notions" on which his "whole life has been based."

Comrade Bell brought many arguments against my thesis, and this was a service, because it enables me to answer my critics in advance. First, what is the value of my memory? Can I be sure that it does not "accommodate itself too easily to the statement Sinclair wishes to believe?" My answer is that few of the important cases in the book rest upon my memory; they rest upon records written down at once. They rest upon drawings which were made according to a plan devised in advance, and then duly filed in envelopes numbered and dated. Also, my memory has been checked by my wife's, who is a fanatic for accuracy, and has caused me torment, through a good part of our married life, by insisting upon going over my manuscripts and censoring every phrase. Also Bob and Dollie and my secretary have read this narrative, and checked the statements dealing with them.

Next objection, that I am "a man without scientific training." The acceptance of that statement depends upon the definition of the word "scientific." If it includes the social sciences, then I have had twenty-five years of very rigid training. I have made investigations and published statements, literally by thousands, which were criminal libels unless they were true and exact; yet I have never had any kind of libel suit brought against me in my life. As to the scientific value of the particular experiments described in this book, the reader can do his own judging, for they have been described in detail. I don't see how scientific training could have increased our precautions. We have outlined our method to scientists, and none has suggested any change.

Next, the fact that in the past I have shown myself "naïve and credulous at times." No doubt I have; but I have learned by such experiences, and I am not so naïve and credulous as when I was younger. Neither do I see how these qualities can play much part in the present matter. I surely know the conditions under which I made my drawings, and whether I had them under my eyes while my wife was making her drawings in another room; I know about the ones I sealed in envelopes, and which were never out of my sight. As for my wife, she certainly has nothing of the qualities of naïveté and credulity. She was raised in a family of lawyers, and was given the training and skeptical point of view of a woman of the world. "Trust people, but watch them," was old Judge Kimbrough's maxim; and following it too closely has almost made a pessimist of his daughter.

Next, that Craig is "in poor health." That is true, but I do not see how it matters here. She has often been in pain, but it has never affected her judgment. She chose her own times for experimenting, when she felt in the mood, and her mind was always clear and keen for the job.

Next, "a husband and wife are a bad pair to make telepathic experiments. Living so much together, their common life does tend to make them think of the same thing at the same time." This is true; but how does it account for the half-dozen successes with a brother-in-law, twenty or thirty with a secretary, and many with Jan? How does it account for the covers and jackets of books in

153

which I had no interest, but which had come to me by chance, and which Craig had never even glanced at, so far as she remembers?

It is true that in the early days most of our drawings were of obvious things which lay about the house, scissors, table-forks, watches, chairs, telephones; so there was a better chance of guess work. How much chance, was determined by my son and his wife, who, hearing that Craig and I were trying telepathy experiments, decided to try a few also—without knowing anything about the technique. They also drew scissors, table-forks, watches, chairs, telephones, and such common objects. The only trouble was that when David tried to reproduce Betty's drawings, he drew the chair where she had drawn the scissors, and drew the watch where she had drawn the table-fork, and so on. They did not get a single success.

I think that if you will go back and look over those drawings as a whole, you must admit that the objects were as varied as the imagination could make them. I do not see how any one could choose a set of objects less likely to be guessed than the series which I have numbered from 5 to 12—a bird's nest full of eggs and surrounded by leaves, a spiked helmet, a desert palm-tree, a star with eight double points, a coconut palm, a puppy chasing a string, a flying bat, a Chinese mandarin, and a boy's foot with a roller-skate on it. None of these objects has any relationship whatever to my life, or to Craig's, or to our common life. To say that a wife can guess such a series, because she knows her husband's mind so well, seems to me out of all reason.

Next, the point that some of the cases are not convincing by themselves. I am familiar with this method of argument, having encountered it with others of my books. Let me beg you to note that the cases are *not* taken by themselves, but are taken as a whole. I can think, for example, of several ways by which Craig might have known that I had put my little paper of written notes into the pocket of my gray coat, or that I had left some medical apparatus under the bathtub at the office. She might have seen these things, and then have forgotten it, and her subconscious mind might have brought back to her the location of the objects, but failed to remind her of the previous seeing. If such cases had

154

stood alone, I would not have thought it worth while to write this book.

The same thing applies to Craig's production of German words. Having spent several weeks with me in Germany, and having known many Germans, she no doubt has German words in her subconscious mind. This also applies to certain dream cases. Any one who wants to can go through the book and pick out a score of cases which can be questioned on various grounds. Perhaps it would be wiser for me to cut out all except the strongest cases. But I rely upon your common sense, to realize that the strongest cases have caused me to write the book; and that the weaker ones are given for whatever additional light they may throw upon the problem.

If you want to deal fairly with the book, here is what you have to explain. How did it happen that at a certain agreed hour when Bob at Pasadena drew a table-fork and dated and signed the drawing, Craig in Long Beach wrote: "See a table-fork, nothing else," and dated and signed her words? If you call this a coincidence, how are you going to account for the chair, and the watch, and the circle with the hole in the middle, and the sense of pain and fear, and the spreading black stain called blood, all reproduced under the same perfect conditions? I say that if you call all this coincidence, you are violating the laws of probability as we know them. I say that there are only two possible explanations, either telepathy, or that my wife and her brother-in-law were hoaxing me.

But if you want to assume a hoax, you have to face the fact that my wife a few days later was reproducing a series of drawings which I made and kept in front of my eyes in a separate room from her, in such a position that she could not see them if she wanted to. If I thought it worth while, I could draw you a diagram of the place where she sat and the place where I sat, and convince you that neither mirrors, nor a hole in the wall, nor any other device would have enabled my wife to see my drawings, until I took them to her and compared them with her drawings. The only way you can account for that series of successes is to say that I am in on the hoax.

My good friend and comrade, Tom Bell, does not suggest that I am in it; but others may say it, so I will answer. Let me assure you, there is no reason in the world why I should take the field on behalf of the doctrine of telepathy—except my conviction that it has been proved. I don't belong to any church which teaches telepathy. I don't hold any doctrine which is helped by it. I don't make any money by advocating or practicing it. There is no more reason why I should be concerned to vindicate telepathy, than there is for my coming out in support of the Catholic doctrine of the Immaculate Conception, or the Mormon doctrine of Urim and Thummim, or the Koreshan doctrine that the earth is a hollow sphere and we live on the inside of it.

I assure you I am as cold-blooded about the thing as a man can be. In fact, I don't like to believe in telepathy, because I don't know what to make of it, and I don't know to what view of the universe it will lead me, and I would a whole lot rather give all my time to my muckraking job which I know by heart. I don't expect to sell especially large quantities of this book; I am sure that by giving the same amount of time and energy to other books I have in mind, I could earn several times as much money. In short, there isn't a thing in the world that leads me to this act, except the conviction which has been forced upon me that telepathy is real, and that loyalty to the nature of the universe makes it necessary for me to say so.

My friend and publisher Charles Boni thinks that I should write this book without protestations; taking a dignified position, sure that my readers will trust me. But as it happens, I have read, not merely the literature of psychic research, but also the literature in opposition to it, and I know the arguments advanced by persons who are unwilling to change their "fundamental notions." It seems common sense to answer here the objections which are certain to be made.

I submitted this manuscript to the two leading psychologists of America, Morton Prince and William McDougall. Dr. Prince was taken by death before he found time to read it, but Professor McDougall read it, and has stated his reactions in the preface. In writing to me, he expressed the hope that my wife would be able to make some of these telepathy tests under the observation of well-known scientists. In replying, I assured him that my wife and I shared this hope; but whether it can ever be realized is a problem for the future. All Craig's work so far has depended upon a state of complete peace and relaxation. As she has pointed out, it is a matter of "undivided concentration," and even such disturbing things as light and noise are an interference. One friend who has tried to experiment lately at our instigation gave it up because of automobile horns in the street outside. She declared that these had never disturbed her before, but that the effort not to hear them when concentrating only caused her to concentrate on the horns, and so threatened to give her a case of "nerves."

Whether Craig would be able to get the necessary state of mind in the presence of strangers, skeptical or possibly hostile, is a problem yet to be solved. Unless we are going to beg the question, we have to assume that telepathy may be a reality; and if it be a reality, then certainly what is in the other person's mind makes a difference, and certainly it is a serious matter to ask a woman in delicate health to open her mind to the moods of strangers. Some day in the future Craig is going to make the test, but whether it succeeds or fails will not alter, so far as I am concerned, what has already happened in my presence.

Another of my friends who read the manuscript was Floyd Dell, and he thinks that readers of my books will wish to know to what extent, if any, my interest in the subject of telepathy is going to change my attitude to the struggle for social justice. To that I reply that I have been interested in psychic research for the past thirty-five years, ever since, as a youth, I met Minot J. Savage; but this has not kept me from believing ardently in the abolition of parasitism, exploitation, and war. While the telepathy experiments were going on I wrote "Boston," a novel of some 325,000 words, in less than a year. While I am consulting with my friends about this manuscript, I am writing a novel, "Mountain City," which I hope my Socialist friends will find of interest. The only discovery that can weaken my interest in the economic problem will be one, which enables human beings to live without food, clothing, and shelter. But in the meantime, I see no reason why Socialists are required to be ignorant of psychology.

James Fuchs, another patient critic of my writings, thinks I appear naïve in this book, and should reveal some knowledge of the vast literature on the subject. My reason for not doing so is that very vastness; one would need several volumes to handle it. In the Proceedings of the American and British Societies for Psychical Research lies buried endless evidence on the subject; but scientific authority remains for the most part uninterested in that evidence, and would not be interested in my rehash of it. I have written this book to tell my readers and friends what I myself have seen with my own eyes. That is my job, and I leave the rest to others who are better qualified.

Fuchs reminds me that "umbilical sensory perception" is a well-known psychic phenomenon, and that Craig, in holding the drawings over her solar plexus, is repeating the method of Justinus Kerner (1786-1862), about whom you will find an article in the "Encyclopedia Britannica." Craig knew about that from various sources, and some of her experiments were designed to test the explanation. I made eight drawings and laid them face down on the table by her couch, perhaps three feet from her head. I put them there while she was out of the room, and I sat and watched, to be sure she did not ever touch them. She lay on the couch and made some notes and drawings which reproduced the essential features of half a dozen of my drawings—all at once! So, if Craig has an umbilical eye, she must also have one in the side of her head which can see through several thicknesses of paper.

My daughter-in-law, Bettina Sinclair, also made suggestions which I accepted. She speaks for the new generation of radicals, saying: "The book aroused a storm of metaphysical speculation in my mind, and I could wax eloquent with slight provocation." This is different from refusing to "abandon the fundamental notions on which my whole life has been based."

XXVI

ONE interesting point I observe: in any company where the subject of this manuscript is brought up, invariably some person declares that he or she has had such experiences. One lady, highly educated, assured me that she and her husband had developed telepathy to a point where it served them on a lonely ranch in the place of telegraph and telephone. Only a few days ago I met at luncheon Bruno Walter, orchestra leader, who had come from Germany to conduct concerts in the Hollywood Bowl. Mr. Walter narrated to me the incident which follows:

While conducting in some middle western city, he was a guest at a luncheon, and found himself becoming very ill. He explained matters to his host, who called a taxicab, but this cab did not arrive, and Mr. Walter, in great distress, took his hat and left the house, saying that he would look for a cab. Turning the corner of the street, he came upon his manager, driving a car, and hailed him. "A most fortunate accident!" exclaimed the sick man, but the manager assured him that it was no accident; about half an hour previously, the manager had been seized by an intense feeling that Mr. Walter was in trouble, and had been moved to get into his car and drive. He did not know where Mr. Walter had gone, but simply followed his impulse to drive in a certain direction.

Another incident, told me by Fremont Older, editor of the San Francisco *Call*, and a veteran fighter in the cause of social justice. Older has seen many demonstrations of telepathy, and is completely convinced of its reality. A friend of his, living on a ranch, employed a cook named Sam who had the gift, and agreed to give a demonstration for the Olders. Sam asked Older to get a book and wrap it in thick paper, and Sam would tell the name of the book and the author. Older went out to his car, but could find no book, only a folder of maps, which he wrapped in several thicknesses of paper. Sam put the package to his head, and after a minute or two said, "This is not a book, it is a map or something. Why don't you get me a regular book?" So Older went to his car again and found a book belonging to his wife, and wrapped it with care and tied it. Sam put it to his head, and began to spell letters, and finally stated as follows: "Julia France and her Times, by Gertrude Atherton, published by the Macmillan Company." This was correct. Sam added: "I get another name. What has Ernest Hopkins got to do with this book?" Older and his wife were dumbfounded; for the name was that of a member of the newspaper staff who had been asked to review the book, but Mrs. Older had taken the copy from him because at the last moment she wanted something to read on her trip.

As this book is going to the printer, my attention is called to the fact that Dr. Carl Bruck of Berlin has published a book entitled "Experimentelle Telepathie," in which he reports a series of tests closely resembling those here described. The main difference is that he used hypnotized subjects, four different young men, as the recipients of his telepathic messages. He made drawings at home, and locked them in a large portfolio, which he placed in an adjoining room from the subject, two or three yards distant through a wall. He himself sat in front of the hypnotized subject, and concentrated upon "sending" one of the drawings. Under these conditions, in a total of 111 experiments, one-third were successful. The Berlin correspondent of the "Scientific American" reported these tests in the issue of May, 1924, where those interested may read the details, and inspect twelve of the drawings. The tests were conducted in the presence of various physicians and scientists; and I am interested in a recent comment on the matter by a German physician living in Mexico City: "Bruck's work has gone almost wholly unnoticed."

I say to scientific men, that such work deserves to be noticed. There is new knowledge here, close to the threshold, waiting for us; and we should not let ourselves be repelled by the seeming triviality of the phenomena, for it is well known that some of the greatest discoveries have come from the following up of just such trivial dews.

What did Benjamin Franklin have to go on when he brought the lightning down from the clouds on the string of a kite? Just a few hints, picked up in the course of the previous hundred years; a few traces of electricity noted by accident. The fact that you got a spark if you stroked a cat's fur; the fact that you got the same kind of a spark by rubbing amber, and a bigger one by storing the energy in a glass jar lined with tinfoil—that was all men had as promise of the miracles of our time, dynamos and superpower, telegraph and telephone, x-ray surgery, radio, wireless, television, and new miracles just outside our door. If now it be a fact that there is a reality behind the notions of telepathy and clairvoyance, to which so many investigators are bearing testimony all over the world, who can set limits to what it may mean to the future? What new powers of the human mind, what ability to explore the past and future, the farthest deeps of space, and those deeps of our own minds, no less vast and marvelous?

To set limits to such possibilities is not to be scientific, it is merely to be foolish. The true scientist sets no limits to human powers, he merely asks that we verify our facts. This my wife and I have tried to do, and I think that, so far as concerns telepathy at least, we can claim success. We present here a mass of real evidence, and we shall not be troubled by any amount of ridicule from the ignorant. I tell you—and because it is so important, I put it in capital letters: TELEPATHY HAPPENS!

For the ultimate in mind expanding and transformational subliminal and self hypnosis programs on CD and MP3, plus consciousness expanding paperbacks and eBooks, visit

www.subliminalselfhypnosis.com

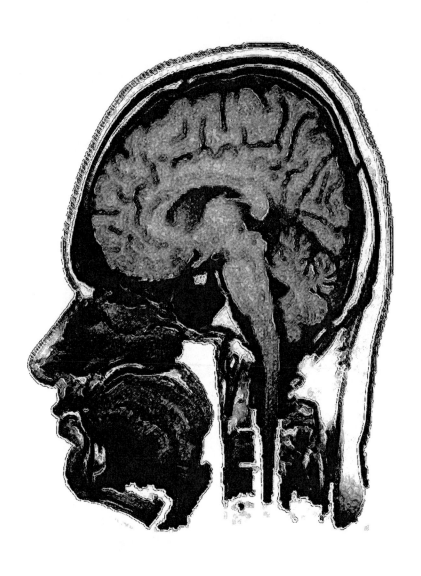

For the ultimate in mind expanding and transformational subliminal and self hypnosis programs on CD and MP3, plus consciousness expanding paperbacks and eBooks, visit

www.subliminalselfhypnosis.com

CPSIA inform
Printed in the U
BVOW08s143122
326623BV00
www.ICGtesting.com
P